MAKE YOUR OWN
HORSE
EQUIPMENT

by
JEAN PERRY

Illustrated by
WILLIAM PERRY

J. A. ALLEN
London

By the same author

Make Your Own Horse Clothing

First published 1984
Reprinted 1986
Reprinted 1989

Published by
J. A. Allen & Company Limited
1 Lower Grosvenor Place, Buckingham Palace Road,
London SW1W 0EL

© Jean Perry, 1984

British Library Cataloguing in Publication Data
Perry, Jean
Make your own horse equipment.
1. Saddlery
I. Title
685'.1   TS1032
ISBN 0–85131–393–0

Printed and bound in Great Britain

CONTENTS

INTRODUCTION

For "Make Your Own Horse Clothing" you had to be able to sew to make those items for your horse or pony. In this book there are only a few for which you need to be able to sew fairly well.

Hopefully, there is something for everyone - for children, for the person who cannot sew a stitch, for those using a needle or sewing machine for the first time, for the experienced needlewoman, and for those who just want to have a go at making something for themselves.

I also hope that one or two mysteries have been cleared up, like "What is the name of that square thing on a headcollar?" and "How do they make a fillet string like that?".

This is by no means an exhaustive list of things you can make for yourself; the popular horse magazines often have suggestions, and you can probably think of more. Besides saving money, finding another use for something you would have thrown away can be satisfying and fun. Often, part of a piece of equipment is beyond redemption, but other parts are not; it would be wasteful to throw away a whole headcollar if the fittings are still good, or a complete lead rope if you can use the clip elsewhere.

Some of the materials need to be bought, and your local market can be a cheap source of many of these. In some cases, the materials listed are only suggestions, and you may find alternatives which suit your needs and pocket better, or even a better way of doing it altogether.

All measurements are given in both imperial and metric units. All metric equivalents are approximate.

SADDLE SEAT COVER

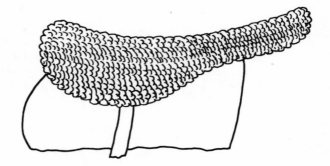

You will need:-

A piece of simulated sheepskin 3 inches (8 cm.) wider than the widest point of your saddle seat, and 4 inches (10 cm.) longer than the distance from the pommel stud to the tip of the cantle.

A piece of ¼ inch (0.75 cm.) thick foam the same size as the simulated sheepskin.

A piece of cotton fabric the same size as the foam and simulated sheepskin.

A piece of ¼ inch (0.75 cm.) wide elastic long enough to pass around the saddle in front of the pommel arch, under the saddle flaps and around the back of the seat.

1¼ yards (1.25 m.) of 1 inch (2.5 cm.) wide tape.

Sewing thread.

To make:-

1. Cut out one piece each of the simulated sheepskin, foam and cotton fabric to the pattern shown.

2. Place the piece of foam on to the wrong side of the simulated sheepskin, and the piece of cotton on top of the foam.

3. Fold ¼ inch (0.75 cm.) of all three layers over to the cotton side, and stitch is down as shown in Fig.1.

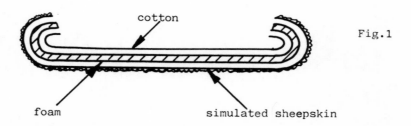

cotton

Fig.1

foam

simulated sheepskin

PATTERN A   —   SADDLE SEAT COVER

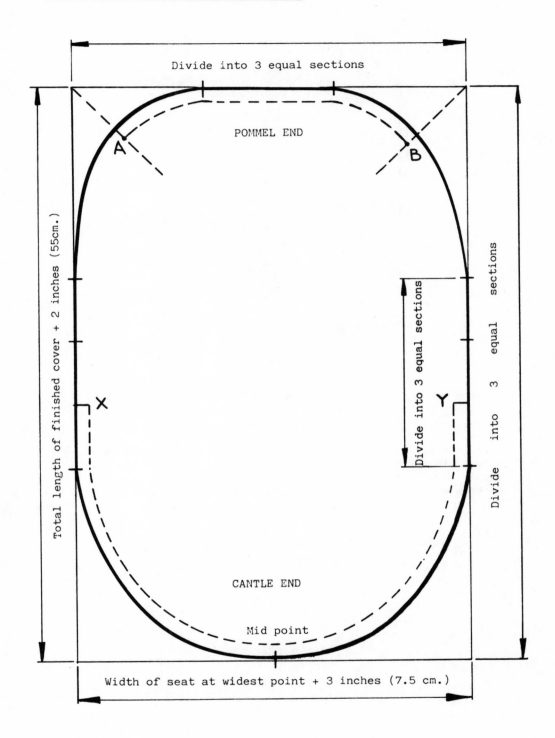

Divide into 3 equal sections

POMMEL END

A

B

Total length of finished cover + 2 inches (55cm.)

Divide into 3 equal sections

Divide into 3 equal sections

X

Y

CANTLE END

Mid point

Width of seat at widest point + 3 inches (7.5 cm.)

4. To form a channel for the elastic, stitch 1 inch (2.5 cm.) wide tape around the pommel end from point A to point B, and round the cantle end from X to Y on the pattern as shown in Fig.2, folding the raw ends of the tape under for neatness.

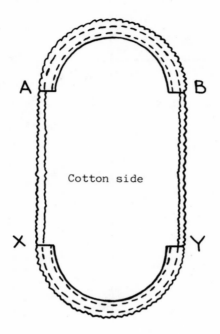

Fig.2

5. Thread elastic through the pommel-end channel from A to B and continue through the cantle-end channel from Y to X. Knot the ends of the elastic together between A and X after fitting the cover to your saddle as follows:-

Place the seat cover on the saddle and slot the right hand saddle flap between the seat cover and the elastic at B to Y and the left hand saddle flap at A to X. Pull the elastic tight enough to keep the seat cover secure and reknot the elastic. Remove the cover from the saddle and cut off the excess elastic. Slide the elastic round so that the knot is inside the channel at the pommel end.

"SKEEPSKIN" NOSEBAND

(The purpose of this is to lower the horse's head if it goes with its nose in the air.)

You will need:-

A piece of ¼ inch (0.75 cm.) thick foam the same length as the part of the noseband to be covered and 3 times its width.

A piece of simulated sheepskin ¼ inch (0.75 cm.) larger all round than the piece of foam.

A strip of 20 mm. wide Velcro touch and close fastening the same length as the foam.

To make:-

1. Place the foam on top of the wrong side of the simulated sheepskin.

2. Fold the edge of the skeepskin over the foam and stitch it in place all the way round.

3. Separate the two pieces of Velcro and stitch one piece along the long side on the pile of the skeepskin, and the other piece of Velcro on the opposite edge, but on the foam side. (Fig.3)

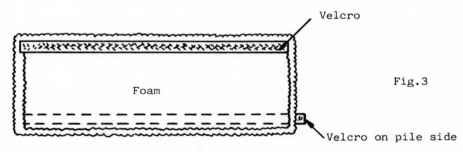

Velcro

Foam

Fig.3

Velcro on pile side

4. Fit the noseband cover around the noseband by wrapping it around and fastening the Velcro on the underside.

5

THREE-COLOURED BROWBAND

You could use velvet, silk or plastic ribbon to cover your browband, although the instructions given are for velvet only.

You will need:-

A browband (an old one will do provided it is sound and clean).

1 length of velvet ribbon the same width as the browband and three times its length.

2 lengths of velvet ribbon each half the width of the browband and three times its length.

Sewing thread.

To make:-

1. Place the two half-width pieces of ribbon side by side and then treat them as one piece of ribbon and the same width as the other (the twin ribbon).

2. Place one end of each piece of ribbon together, with the velvet sides outermost, and stitch them together at an angle of 60° about 1 inch (2.5 cm.) from the end. (Fig.4)

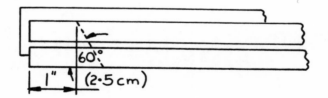

Fig.4

3. With the outer side of the browband facing you place the browband between the ribbons as shown in Fig.5.

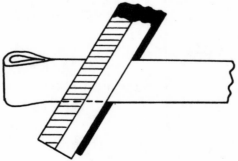

Fig.5

4. Fold the twin ribbon over and down between the browband and the single ribbon. (Fig.6)

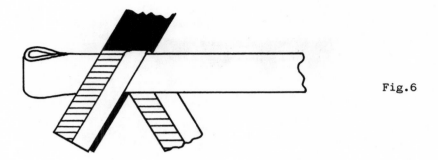

Fig.6

5. Fold the single ribbon over, down, under and up, so that it covers the twin ribbon at the front, and passes between it and the browband at the back. Always finish with the single ribbon pointing upwards. (Fig.7)

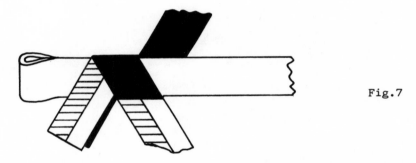

Fig.7

6. Fold the twin ribbon under, up, over and down, so that it covers the single ribbon at the front and passes between it and the browband at the back. Always finish with the twin ribbon pointing downwards. (Fig.8)

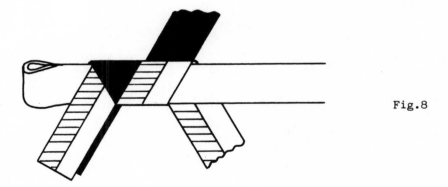

Fig.8

7. Repeat steps 5 and 6 until the twin ribbon reaches the end of the browband.

8. Fold the single ribbon over and down. Stitch the ends of the ribbons
   together and cut notches to stop them fraying. (Fig.9)

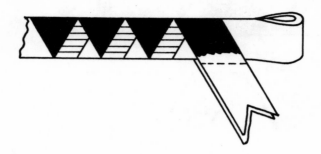

Fig.9

DIAMOND-PATTERNED COLOURED BROWBAND

You will need:-

A browband (an old one will do provided it is sound and clean).

Velvet ribbon fractionally wider than the browband and 6 times its length in one colour, and the same amount in another colour (referred to here as black and white).

Sewing thread.

To make:-

1. Cut each piece of ribbon in half so that you have 2 pieces of each colour and all 4 pieces the same length.

2. Place one end of a piece of black and one end of a piece of white together, with the velvet sides outermost, and stitch them together at an angle of 45° about 1 inch (2.5 cm.) from the end. (Fig.10)

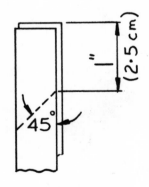

Fig.10

3. Repeat with the other 2 pieces of ribbon.

4. Hold the browband vertically, and place it between one pair of ribbons as shown in Fig.11.

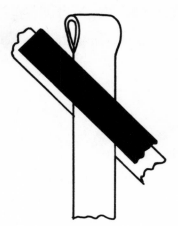

Fig.11

5. Decide which colour you want to appear as the diamond in the centre of the browband (shown here as white), and place the other pair of ribbons over both the browband and the first pair of ribbons so that the white ribbon is on top of the black at the back as well as the front. There should be one black and one white ribbon at the back, and one black and one white at the front (Fig.12).

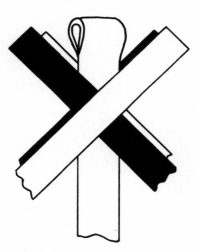

Fig.12

6. Winding both the white ribbons in one direction and both the black in the other, follow the stages shown in Fig.13 (Steps I - IV) and repeat this sequence until the length of the browband has been covered.

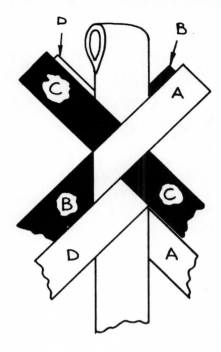 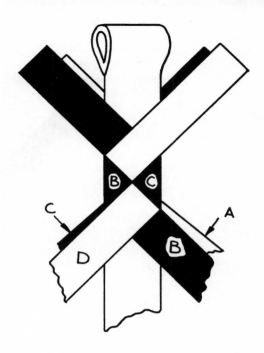

(I) Pass white ribbon A round to the back under Black B, and White D round to the front under Black C.

(II) Pass Black B across the front under White D, and Black C across the back under White A.

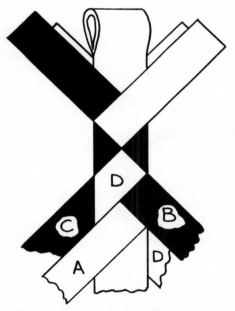 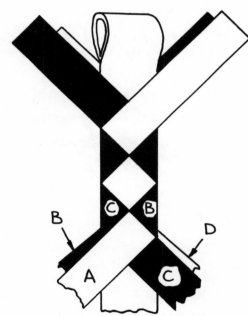

(III) Pass White D round the back under Black C, and White A across the front under Black B.

(IV) Pass Black C across the front under White A, and Black B round the back under White D.

Fig. 13

11

7. When the length of the browband has been covered, end as you began, with one black and one white ribbon together at each side of the vertical browband. (Fig.14)

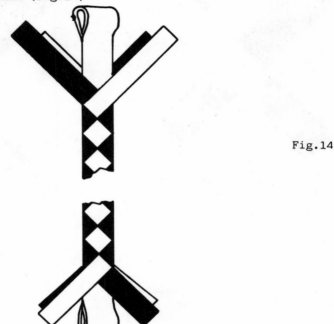

Fig.14

8. With the browband horizontal, fold the ends of ribbon at the top (X and Y), down to the back and stitch all four ends firmly together. (Fig.15)

Fig.15

9. Cut notches in the ends of the ribbons to stop them fraying.

To Make A Browband With Alternate Diamonds In A Different Colour:-

Replace one of the white ribbons with another colour, and refer to this as either A or D in Fig.13.

GIRTH SLEEVE

You will need:-

A piece of simulated sheepskin 9 inches (23 cm.) wide and the length of
   your girth, excluding the buckles.

Sewing thread.

To make:-

1. Fold the fabric in half down its length with the pile side inside.

2. Make this into a tube by sewing the raw edges together down the long
   side, with a row of stitching ½ inch (1.25 cm.) from the edge.

3. Turn the tube through so that the pile side is now on the outside.

4. Slide the tube over your girth, making sure that the seam is on the
   flat side of the girth which is not next to the horse.

GIRTH BUCKLE GUARDS

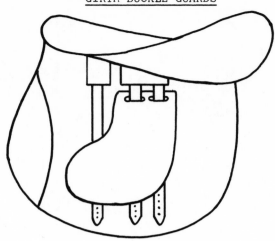

You will need:-

2 pieces of stout leather each 6 inches (15 cm.) x 10 inches (25 cm.)

A sharp modelling knife and a metal straight edge <u>or</u> a woodworker's chisel the same width as your girth straps.

Hole punch, linen thread, harness needle and leather awl.

Leather dye if the leather is not already dyed.

To make:-

1. Cut out the two pieces of leather as a pair to the pattern shown.

2. Place one piece of leather over the back two girth straps on one side of your saddle, with the short straight edge at the top as shown in Fig.14, and mark the position of the slots along this straight edge.

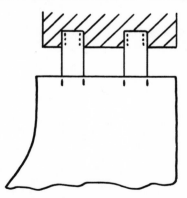

Fig.14

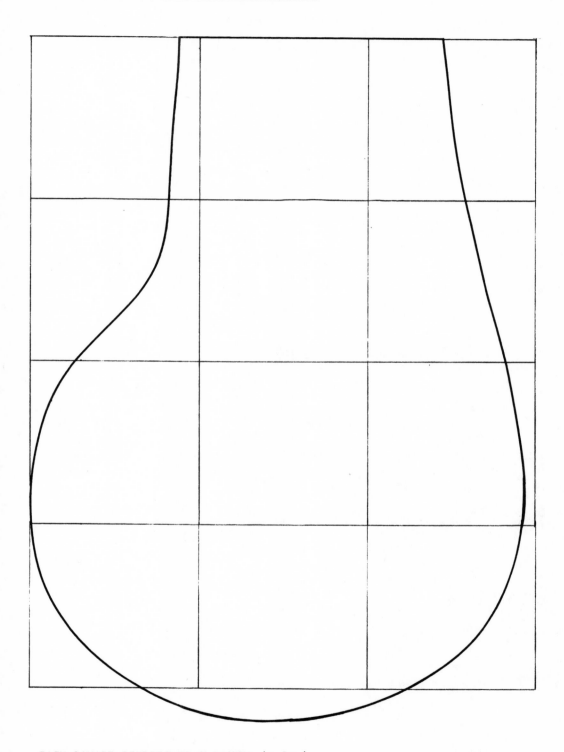

EACH SQUARE REPRESENTS 2 INCHES (5 CM.)
CUT AROUND SOLID LINE ONLY.

3. Punch a hole at each of these 4 positions approximately 1 inch (2.5 cm.) down from the top edge.

4. Cut between each pair of holes using the modelling knife or chisel. (Fig.1

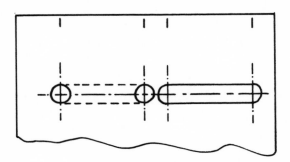

Fig.15

5. If the leather needs dying, apply dye to the top surface only so that no dye will come off on to your girth.

6. Slide the two back girth straps through the slots in the top of the guard so that the straps end up underneath.

7. Make holes in the top of the guards with the awl and stitch the guard to the girth webbing of your saddle. Use large, tacking type stitches so that the edge of the guard just meets the edge of the girth webbing. This will ensure that there are no uncomfortable bulges in your saddle flap. (Fig. 16)

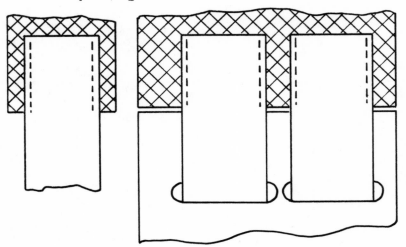

Fig.16

HOOF PICK CASE
(To tie on your saddle)

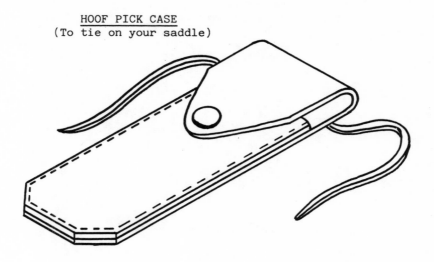

You will need:-

A piece of soft leather 2 inches (5 cm.) wide x 13 inches (33 cm.) long.

A leather bootlace or thong.

A hammer-on type of press stud or a button with a shank.

To make:-

1. Place the hoof pick on the piece of leather and fold the leather as shown in Fig.17

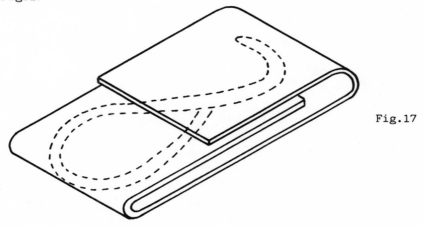

Fig.17

2. Cut off the lower folded corners, and cut the flap to the shape you require.

17

3. Mark the position of the centre of each of the two halves of the press stud or the centre of the button and buttonhole.

4. Unfold the leather from the hoof pick, and attach the two halves of the press stud, or sew on the button and cut a slot for the button hole.

5. Stitch the side seams together, and punch two holes through which to thread the bootlace or thong. (Fig.18)

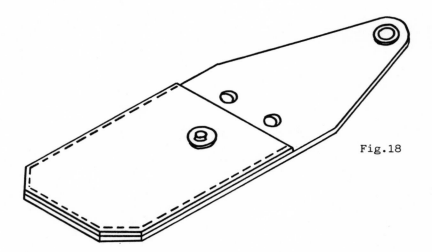

Fig.18

6. Thread the bootlace through the two holes and tie the hoof pick in its case to one of the D rings at the front of your saddle.

NOTE: This will hold either the plastic or metal type of hoof pick without a brush. To make a case for the larger type of hoof pick with a brush you will need a piece of leather approximately 4½ inches (12 cm.) wide by 18 inches (46 cm.) long.

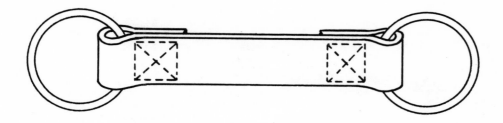

You will need;-

2 metal rings each 1½ inches (4 cm.)in diameter.

A strip of nylon webbing or strap leather 1 inch (2.5 cm.) wide x 9 inches (23 cm.) long

Suitable thread for sewing.

To make:-

1. Fold 2 inches (5 cm.) at one end of the strip of webbing or leather around one of the rings and stitch it in place as shown in Fig.19. (To fold leather without it cracking, dip the portion to be folded into water to soften the fibres.)

Leather

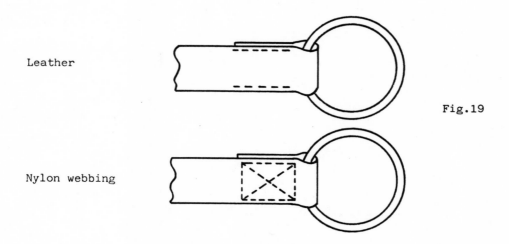

Nylon webbing

Fig.19

2. Repeat with the other ring.

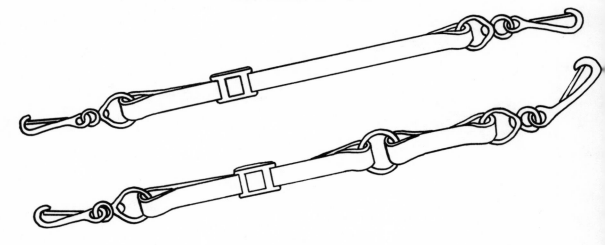

You will need:-

For a pair of grass reins:-

3 yards (3 m.) of 1 inch (2.5 cm.) wide nylon webbing.

2 x 1 inch (2.5 cm.) Roko buckles.

4 billet hooks (spring clips).

Additionally, for a pair of side reins:-

2 Peacock (safety) stirrup rings.

To make grass reins:-

1. Cut the nylon webbing into two equal lengths and seal the ends by passing them through a flame.

2. Thread one end of one of the pieces over the centre bar of a Roko buckle so that the longest end protrudes from the bar end of the buckle, and stitch it in place around the bar as shown in Fig. 20.

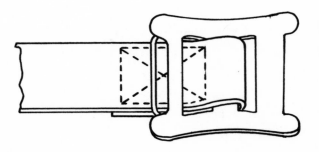

Fig.20

3. Pass the free end of the webbing through the ring of one of the billet hooks, and then under the buckle bar and through the buckle. (Fig.21)

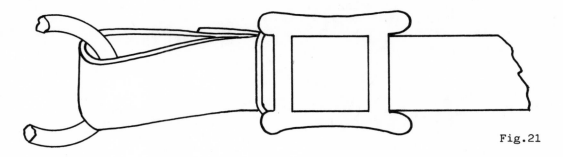

Fig.21

4. Stitch the free end of the webbing around the ring of another billet hook. (Fig.22)

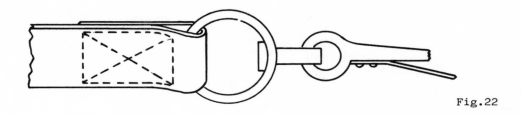

Fig.22

5. Make another rein to match the first.

To make side reins:-

Carry out steps 1 to 5 for side reins.

6. Cut through the webbing about 8 inches (20 cm.) from the fixed hook end, and seal the cut edges.

7. Fold the sealed ends around one of the Peacock stirrup rings and stitch them in place as shown in Fig.23.

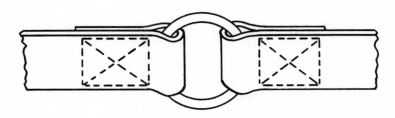

Fig.23

21

NYLON HEADCOLLAR

The instructions are for a headcollar made with nickel plated fittings and
Roko buckles. The changes which need to be made for one with a pinned buckle
and eyelets can be found at the end of this section. Brass fittings could
also be used.

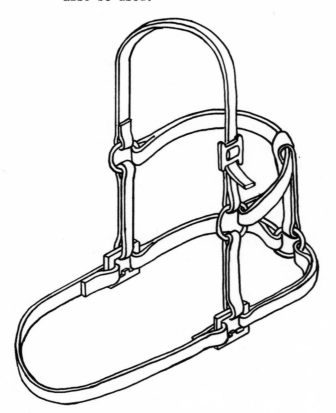

Instructions are given for
three styles:

(A) Non-adjustable, with single
thickness over nose and head

(B) Non-adjustable with double
thickness throughout.

(C) Adjustable over the nose,
with double thickness
throughout.

Finished measurements

Size	* Over nose in.(cm.)	Under chin in.(cm.)	Cheeks in.(cm.)	Throat-latch in.(cm.)	Throat to chin in.(cm.)	Head-piece in.(cm.)	Buckle-piece in.(cm.)
Shetland	10½(26)	4 (10)	5 (12.75)	12(30.5)	4½(11.5)	22(56)	3 (7.5)
Pony	12½(32)	4½(11.5)	5½(14)	13(33)	5 (12.75)	24(61)	3 (7.5)
Cob	14½(37)	5 (12.5)	6¼(16)	14(35.5)	5¾(15)	25(63.5)	3 (7.5)
Full	16½(42)	5½(14)	7 (17.75)	15(38)	6½(16.5)	28(71)	3½(9)

* The over nose measurement in Style (c) is adjustable.

You will need:-

A packet of small self-adhesive labels.

Strong thread to match the nylon webbing.

Materials	(A) Non-adjustable with single thickness over nose and head.	(B) Non-adjustable with double thickness throughout.	(C) Adjustable noseband with double thick- ness throughout
1"(2.5 cm.) Roko buckle.	1	1	2
1"(2.5 cm. x 1¼"(3 cm.) stop square.	2	2	2
1½"(4 cm.) diameter metal ring.	3	3	3
Nylon webbing: Shetland 1"(2.5 cm.) wide.	3½ yds.(3.25 m.)	4¼ yds.(4 m.)	4½ yds.(4.25 m)
Pony	3¾ yds.(3.5 m.)	4⅔ yds.(4.25 m.)	5 yds.(4.5 m.)
Cob	4 yds.(3.75 m.)	5¼ yds.(4.75 m.)	5⅔ yds.(5 m.)
Full	4½ yds.(4 m.)	5⅔ yds.(5.25 m.)	6 yds.(5.5 m.)

To Make:-

1. Write the name of each piece of the headcollar on an adhesive label (two each for "under chin" and "cheek"), and stick them on to the nylon webbing as you cut it.

2. Cut the webbing into the lengths shown in the following tables, and seal the cut ends by passing them through a flame.

For all styles

Piece	Under chin	Cheeks	Throatlatch	Throat to chin	Buckle piece
No. to cut	2	2	1	1	1
Shetland	9(23)	11 (28)	25(63.5)	10 (25.5)	8(20)
Pony	10(25.5)	12 (30.5)	27(68.5)	11 (28)	8(20)
Cob	11(28)	13½(34)	29(73.5)	12½(32)	8(20)
Full	12(30.5)	15 (37)	31(78.5)	14 (35.5)	9(23)

Measurements are shown in inches with their metric equivalent shown in brackets.

Cut one of each of the following pieces for the style you have chosen.

	Over nose	Nose buckle piece	Headpiece
STYLE (A): Shetland	14½(37)	–	24(61)
Pony	16½(42)	–	26(66)
Cob	18½(47)	–	27(70)
Full	20½(52)	–	30(76)
STYLE (B): Shetland	22½(57)	–	45(114)
Pony	26 (66)	–	49(124)
Cob	30 (76)	–	51(130)
Full	34 (86)	–	57(145)
STYLE (C): Shetland	25 (63.5)	8(20)	45(114)
Pony	29 (74)	8(20)	49(124)
Cob	33 (84)	8(20)	51(130)
Full	37 (94)	9(23)	57(145)

3. For style (A), fold 1 inch (2.5 cm.) at each end of the nosepiece around a stop square and stitch in place as shown in Fig.24.

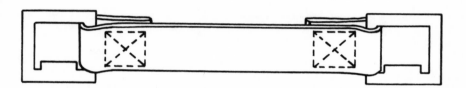

Fig.24

For Style (B), thread the nosepiece through the two stop squares and overlap the ends by 1 inch (2.5 cm.). Stitch as shown in Fig.25.

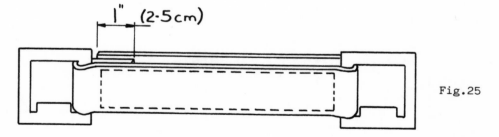

Fig.25

For Style (C), thread the nose buckle piece around the centre bar of one of the Roko buckles and one of the stop squares, and stitch as shown in Fig.26.

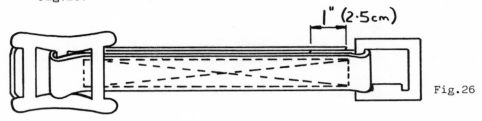

1" (2.5cm)

Fig.26

Wrap the over nose piece around the other stop square, overlapping the ends by 1 inch (2.5 cm.), and stitch as shown in Fig.27.

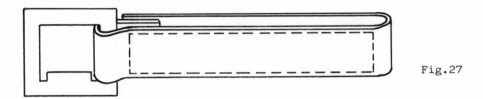

Fig.27

Do up the buckle over the nose to make it easier to make the rest of the headcollar.

4. For all styles, pass one of the under chin pieces round one stop square and one ring. Overlap the ends by 1 inch (2.5 cm.) and stitch. (Fig.28)

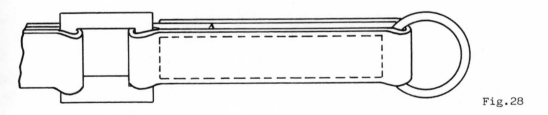

Fig.28

5. Fix the other under chin piece round the same ring and the other stop square to form a circle round the nose and stitch in the same way. (Fig.29)

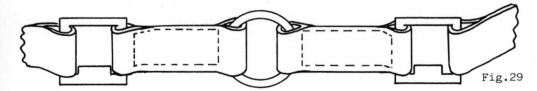

Fig.29

6. Using the same method as for the under chin pieces, attach the cheek pieces, joining the top of each stop square to the remaining two rings. (Fig.30)

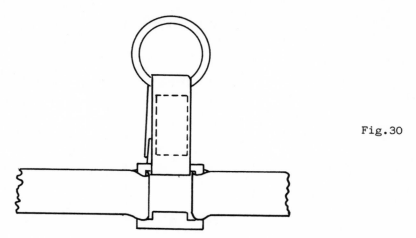

Fig.30

7. Join these last two rings together with the throatlatch piece in the same way. (Fig.31)

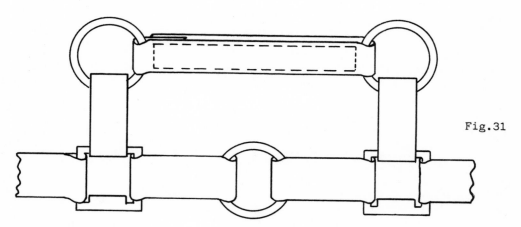

Fig.31

8. Connect the throatlatch to the under chin ring. (Fig.32)

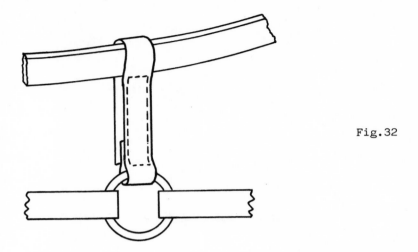

Fig.32

9. Fit the head piece to the right hand cheek ring by folding 1 inch (2.5 cm.)
   at one end around the ring and stitching as shown in Fig.33 for Style (A),
   or threading the headpiece around the ring and overlapping the ends by
   1 inch (2.5 cm.) before stitching for Styles (B) and (C). (Fig.34)

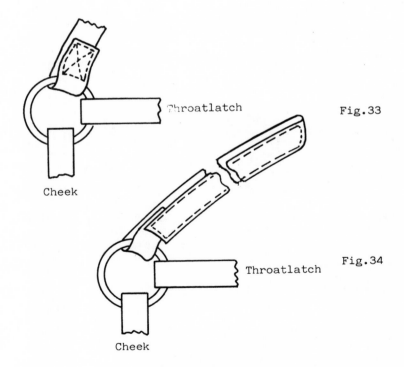

Throatlatch   Fig.33

Cheek

Throatlatch   Fig.34

Cheek

10. Pass the remaining piece of webbing around the centre bar of the Roko buckle and the left hand cheek ring. Overlap the ends by 1 inch (2.5 cm.) and stitch as shown in Fig.35.

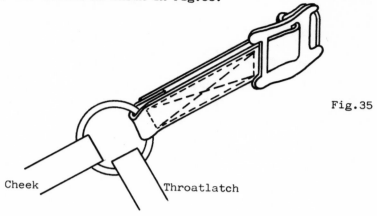

Fig.35

Cheek   Throatlatch

To make a headcollar with a pinned buckle and eyelets

When fitting buckles with a pin in place of Roko buckles, burn two holes and cut a slot in the nylon webbing before fitting the buckle. Use a steel knitting needle or a nail which has been heated to do this. HOLD THE NAIL OR KNITTING NEEDLE IN A PAIR OF PLIERS SO THAT YOU DO NOT BURN YOURSELF. (Fig.36)

Fig.36

Slot the webbing over the pin of the buckle and then around the stop square or ring. (Fig.37)

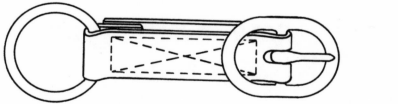

Fig.37

When the headcollar is complete, make holes in the corresponding strap either by burning or with a sharp hole punch. Eyelets of a suitable size for the buckle pin can then be fitted using an eyelet tool. (Fig.38)

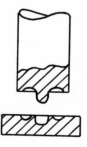

Fig.38

28

LUNGEING CAVESSON

With this type of cavesson the lunge rein must either have a swivel clip or have a separate swivel inserted into the webbing near the clip.

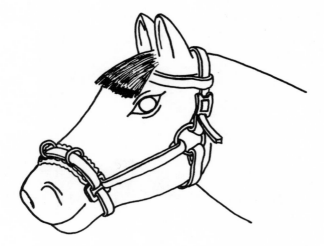

You will need:-

A nylon headcollar or the materials to make one, not adjustable over the nose.

A piece of nylon webbing long enough to make a browband (i.e. the length of the browband plus 4 inches (10 cm.)

A piece of nylon webbing the same length as the over nose piece of the headcollar, and 1 inch (2.5 cm.)wide.

A piece of sheepskin the same length as the over nose piece of the headcollar and 1 inch (2.5 cm.) wider.

3 x 1 inch (2.5 cm.) 'D' rings.

A whole roller buckle (pinned) the same width as the nylon webbing of the headcollar.

Strong thread to match the nylon webbing.

To make:-

1. Make a headcollar without nose adjustment, but omit the following stages from the instructions for making a headcollar:

    Steps 4 and 5 - Fixing the nylon webbing to the stop squares and ring under the chin.

    Step 8   - Connecting the throatlatch to the under chin ring.

    OR Unpick and remove the under chin pieces of webbing and ring,and the webbing connecting the throatlatch to the under chin ring.

2. Place the three 'D' rings on the headcollar noseband, positioned as shown in Fig.39, and secure them in place by stitching as shown on the outside of the noseband.

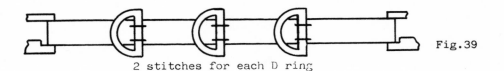

2 stitches for each D ring

Fig.39

3. Thread the piece of nylon webbing which is the same length as the over nose piece of the headcollar through the 'D' rings and stitch this securely. (Fig.40)

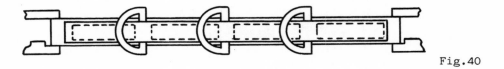

Fig.40

4. Place the piece of sheepskin on the underside of the noseband with the pile side next to the horse's nose and hand stitch this at the edge of the nylon webbing. (Fig.41)

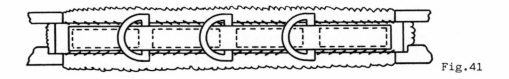

Fig.41

5. Attach one of the under chin pieces of webbing to one of the stop squares, but with a buckle where the ring would normally go on a headcollar. (Fig.42)

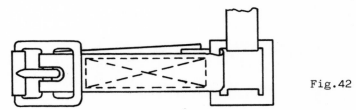

Fig.42

6. Fold 1 inch (2.5 cm.) at the end of the other under chin piece round the other stop square and stitch this in place. Make holes for the buckle pin with a hole punch and then fit eyelets, or use a hot nail or knitting needle to pierce holes which will not need eyelets. (Fig.43)

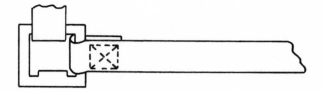

Fig.43

7. Do up the buckle under the chin. Fold the piece of webbing which is to connect the throatlatch with this around the throatlatch and the under chin piece, and stitch it so that both parts can slide through the loops in the ends. (Fig.44)

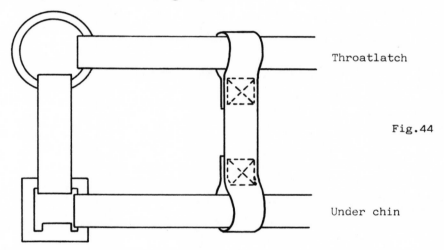

Throatlatch

Fig.44

Under chin

8. Make a browband from the remaining piece of nylon webbing as shown in Fig.45 and thread this on to the headpiece of the cavesson.

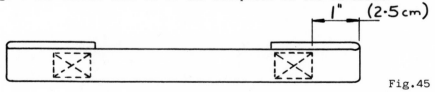

1" (2·5 cm)

Fig.45

LUNGE WHIP

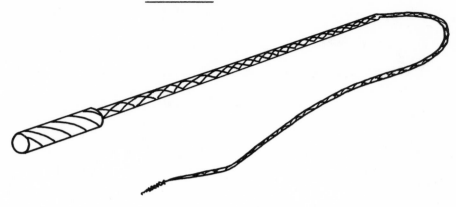

You will need:-

A thin garden cane 6 feet (2 m.) long or the top section of an old fibreglass
fishing rod if this is long enough.

An old haynet of the tubular nylon plaited type.

A strip of leather or towelling 1 inch (2.5 cm.) wide x 24 inches (61 cm.) long

Glue which will stick the leather or towelling to the cane or fibreglass.

1½ yds. (1.5 m.) thick linen thread.

To make:-

1. Unknot the haynet until you have a length of good tubular nylon about
   14 feet (13 m.) long.

2. Open out the tube at one end of the tubular nylon and slide it over the
   thinnest end of the garden cane or fishing rod, and all the way down over
   it to the thickest end. (Fig.46)

Fig.46

32

3. Place one end of the strip of leather or towelling across the thick end of the cane or rod and then bind about 7 inches (18 cm.) at this end to form a handle. Glue the leather or towelling in place as you bind. (Fig.47)

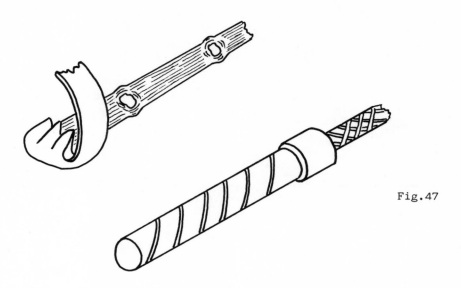

Fig.47

4. Fold the free end of tubular nylon down alongside the cane or rod, and cut off the end so that the lash part of the whip is the same length as the rigid part. (Fig.48)

Cut

Fig.48

5. Cut off 6 inches (15 cm.) of thread and place this on one side.

6. Fold the remaining, longer piece of thread in half and then in half again. Hold one end of the bundle of 4 strands of thread firmly, and twist the other end until kinks appear in the twisted thread. Keeping the twisted thread pulled tight, fold it in half and then let the folded end go so that a short cord is formed by the thread naturally twisting itself.

7. Using the short piece of thread which you had cut off and placed on one side, bind the unfolded end of the cord to the free end of the lash. Tie two or three knots in the cord. (Fig.49)

Fig.49

34

LUNGE REIN/LEAD REIN

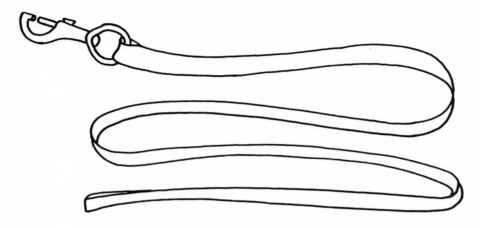

You will need:-

7 yds. (6.5 m.) of nylon or thick cotton webbing for a lunge rein.

2¼ yds. (2 m.) of nylon webbing for a lead rein.

A large spring clip for both types of rein, and strong thread.

A rope swivel for the lunge rein if the spring clip is not the swivel type.

To make:-

1. If nylon webbing is being used, seal the cut ends by passing them through a flame.

2. Fold 1½ inches (4 cm.) at one end of the webbing around the eye of the spring clip and stitch as shown in Fig.50.

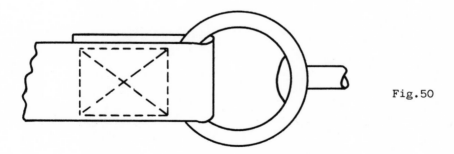

Fig.50

3. Fold 9 inches (23 cm.) at the other end of the webbing into a loop and stitch as shown in Fig.51.

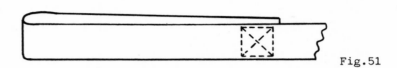

Fig.51

4. If the spring clip is not of the swivel type, insert a rope swivel into the lunge rein about 10 inches (25 cm.) from the clip as shown in Fig.52. Seal the cut ends before stitching.

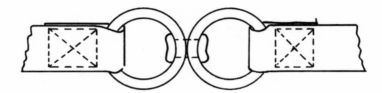

Fig.52

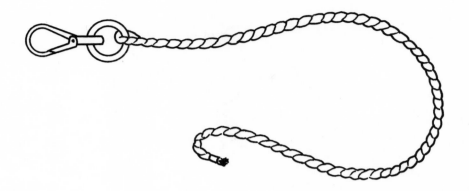

You will need:-

A large spring clip (possibly salvaged from an old lead rope).

2⅛ yds. (2 m.) of 3 strand rope (available from boat chandlers or outdoor
   pursuit shops.

4 inches (10 cm.) self-adhesive carpet tape.

To make:-

1. Unwind the three strands at one end of the rope for about 4 inches (10 cm.)
   and pass these strands through the eye of the spring clip. Fold this
   end of the rope so that the part which has not been unravelled is around
   the eye, and the three strands are positioned as shown in Fig.53.

   Strand B is the central strand.
   Strand A emerges from the under side of the rope, and is to the left.
   Strand C from the upper side of the rope is to the right.

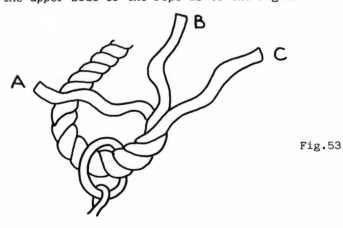

Fig.53

2. Tuck strand B under one of the twists in the main part of the rope close to the eye, and point it to the right. (Fig. 54)

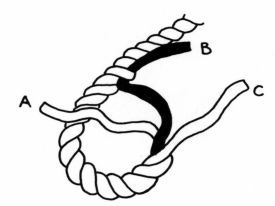

Fig. 54

3. Pass strand A over the twist under which strand B was tucked, and then under the next twist in the rope. Leave strand A pointing to the left. (Fig. 55)

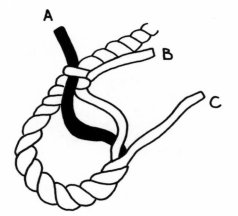

Fig. 55

4. Pull strands A and B tight, and turn the work over so that strand A is now on the right and B and C on the left.

5. Pass strand C across the top of the rope to the right, and then to the left under the next twist of the rope. (Fig.56) Pull strand C tight.

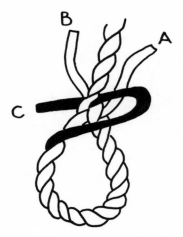

Fig.56

You should now have one strand emerging from between each twist of the rope.

6. Following the sequence B, A, C, tuck each strand in turn over the next twist of the rope and under the next, until the ends of the strands have been reached. Cut the ends of the strands close to the twists of the rope. The completed eye splice should look like Fig.57, and the **harder** the rope is pulled, the tighter the splice becomes.

Fig.57

7. Bind the free end of the rope with adhesive carpet tape to stop it from fraying. (Fig.58)

Fig.58

39

LEAD ROPE (2)
(home-made rope)

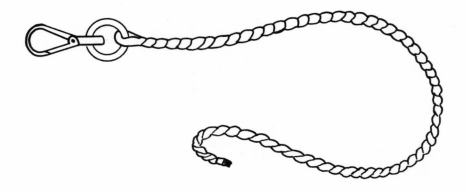

You will need:-

2 other people to help you.

A hand drill with a bent nail in place of the drill bit.

3 pencils.

A large spring clip.

6 strands each 12 yds.(11 m.) long of white parcel string or other yarn strong enough to make a rope.

A tin of Dylon fabric dye if the yarn or string is not already the colour of your choice.

16 inches (46 cm.) self-adhesive carpet tape.

A LOT OF ROOM!

To make:-

1. Make a bundle of three strands of string each 12 yds.(11 m.) long. Fold the bundle in half, and insert a pencil through the loop formed at the fold. Ask friend A to hold the pencil.

2. Tie a knot at the other end and hook this over the bent nail in the hand drill. Keeping the string tight, turn the drill handle to twist the strands together until kinks appear. (Fig.59)

Fig.59

3. Ask friend B to hold the string at the centre by holding a pencil vertically against it, and to keep the string tight.

4. Walk to meet friend A and take the end of the string and the pencil from her. Hold this end next to the end over the bent nail. Ask friend B to make sure that the pencil is trapped in the loop which has formed at her end and to then let go of her end.

5. When the string has naturally twisted itself into a cord, use a short piece (about 4 inches (10 cm.)) of carpet tape to hold the ends nearest you together. Remove the pencil and bent nail from the cord at your end.

6. Make a second cord in the same way from the other three strands of string.

7. Place the two cords side by side with their pencils at the same end. Pass one pencil through both loops - remove the other.

8. Knot the other ends together and hook this knot over the bent nail in the drill. Twist the two cords together in the same way as you made them, but ask friend B to hold the spring clip and to straighten out the kinks in the centre before you walk to meet friend A.

9. Friend B should remove the pencil from the loop she is holding and pass this fold through the eye of the spring clip. (Fig.60) SHE SHOULD NOT LET GO OF HER END.

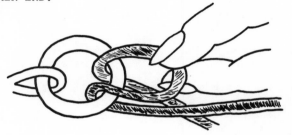

Fig.60

10. Tape together the ends which you and friend A are holding. Remove the pencil and bent nail from your end, and let go.

11. When the cords have naturally twisted themselves into a rope, insert the free end into the loop which is through the eye and pull the rope tight. (Fig.61)

Fig.61

12. Retape the free end at a neat point **closest** to the end and trim to tidy it up.

BASHING BAG

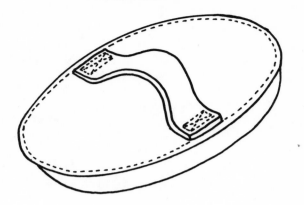

You will need:-

2 pieces of soft leather or suede each about 5 inches (12.5 cm.) x 8 inches
   (20 cm.).

1 piece of leather or suede about 5 inches (12.5 cm.) x 1 inch (2.5 cm.)

Soft toy stuffing or old nylon tights with the feet and waistbands cut off.

Strong thread.

To make:-

1. Cut out the three pieces of leather or suede as shown on the pattern.

2. Stitch the two ends of the leather strip on to one of the oval leather
   pieces as shown in Fig. 62.

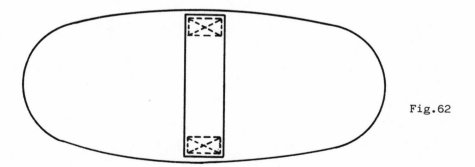

Fig.62

3. Place this oval shape on top of the other, with the stitched on strip
   on the outside. Stitch these pieces together around the edge, but
   leave one end open for stuffing. (Fig.63)

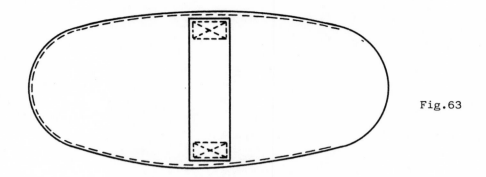

Fig.63

4. Stuff between the two layers until you can get no more in. Stitch the
open end closed.

PATTERN C   —   BASHING BAG

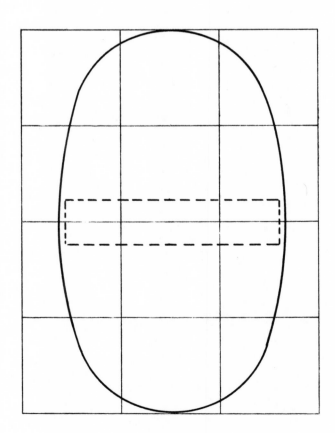

EACH SQUARE REPRESENTS 2 INCHES (5 CM.)
CUT AROUND SOLID LINE ONLY.

GROOMING MITT

You will need:-

A piece of paper sufficiently large to make a pattern of your hand.

A pencil.

2 pieces of real or simulated sheepskin just larger than your hand.

Strong thread.

To make:-

1. Place your hand on the piece of paper and draw an outline round it about
   1 inch (2.5 cm.) larger all the way round. (Fig. 64)

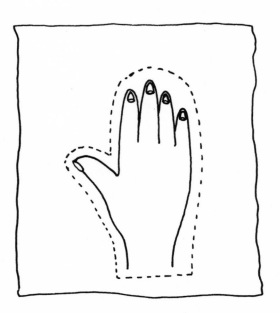

Fig.64

2. Place the right sides of the real or simulated sheepskin together and cut them out to the pattern you have made.

3. Leave the wrist edge open, and stitch the two pieces together around the remaining edges. (Fig. 65)

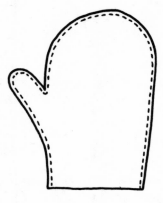

Fig.65

4. Turn the mitt through to the right side.

REVERSIBLE WAISTCOAT

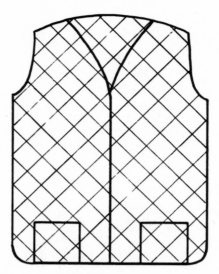

First take the following measurements:

(A) Chest or bust measurement over the type of clothing you would wear with this garment.

(b) The distance from the neck edge of your shoulder seam to the lower hem of the waistcoat to be made.

You will need:-

A piece of double sided quilted fabric (or you could quilt your own) of width:measurement (A) + 3 inches (7.5 cm.) and length: measurement (B) + 1 inch (2.5 cm.).

Sufficient 20 mm. wide Velcro touch and close fastening to match the length of the front opening.

½inch (1.25 cn.) wide bias binding in a matching or contrasting colour long enough to bind the edges of the front opening, neck edge, lower hem, armholes and four pocket tops. (5½ yds. (5 m.) should be enough for a 36 inch (92 cm.) bust.)

Sewing thread.

To make:-

1. Cut out one main piece and four pockets according to the pattern.

2. Bind the top edges of the pockets as shown in Fig. 66.

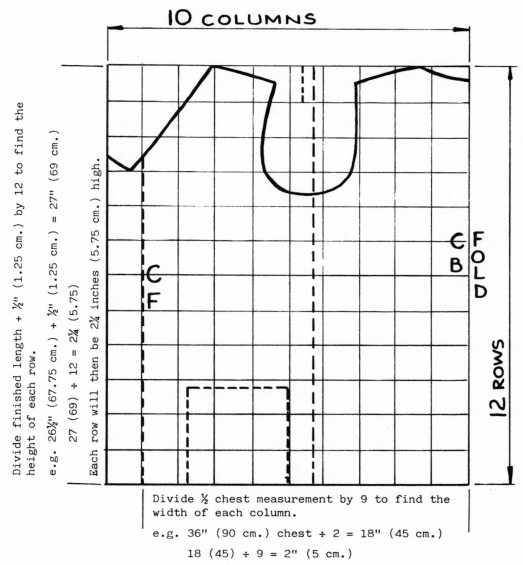

Divide finished length + ½" (1.25 cm.) by 12 to find the height of each row.

e.g. 26½" (67.75 cm.) + ½" (1.25 cm.) = 27" (69 cm.)

27 (69) ÷ 12 = 2¼ (5.75)

Each row will then be 2¼ inches (5.75 cm.) high.

Divide ½ chest measurement by 9 to find the width of each column.

e.g. 36" (90 cm.) chest ÷ 2 = 18" (45 cm.)

18 (45) ÷ 9 = 2" (5 cm.)

Each column will then be 2 inches (5 cm.) wide.

CUT AROUND SOLID LINE ONLY.

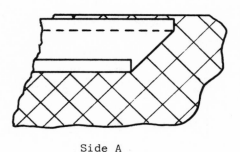
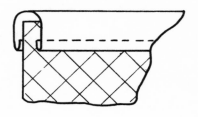

Side A   Side B

Fig.66

3. Fold ½ inch (1.25 cm.) under to the wrong side down the side edges only
   of all four pockets, and tack the folds in place. Place two of the pocket
   at the position shown on the pattern on one side of the main piece
   of fabric and tack them in place around all four sides. (Fig.67)

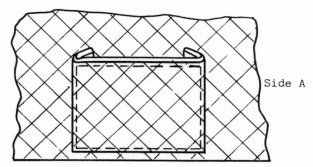

Side A

Fig.67

4. Pin the other two pockets on the other side of the material in exactly
   the same position as the first two. When you are sure that that they
   are positioned correctly, tack them in place with stitches that pass
   through all three layers of material. (Fig.68)

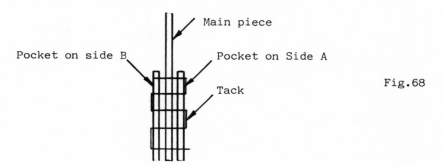

Main piece

Pocket on side B   Pocket on Side A

Tack

Fig.68

5. Machine stitch the pockets down both sides and along the lower edge,
   through all layers. Remove all the tacking stitches. (Fig.69)

48

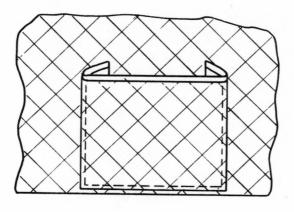

Fig.69

6. Join the shoulders with a machine fell seam as shown in Fig.70.

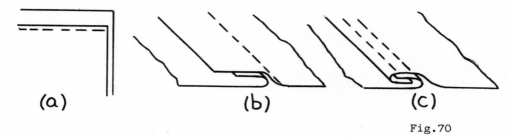

(a)   (b)   (c)

Fig.70

7. Run a row of machine stitching around all raw edges, close to the edge, to hold the filling and layers of material together. This will make the following steps easier.

8. Separate the two halves of Velcro, and place one piece, with its sticking face up, along the front opening on one side of the fabric so that it overlaps the raw edge by ¼ inch (0.75 cm.), and tack this in place. Put the other piece of Velcro in the corresponding position on <u>the other side of the fabric</u> and tack this (i.e. one piece of Velcro will be on the outside of the work, and the other piece will be on the inside).(Fig.71)

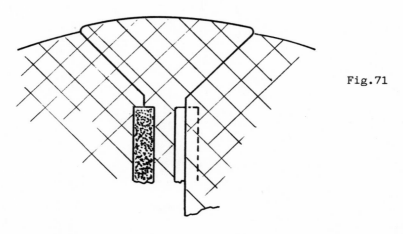

Fig.71

49

9. Fold one front edge in and one front edge out, so that the sticky sides of the Velcro are still visible, and the edge of the Velcro is about ⅜ inch (1 cm.) from the fold. Tack and then machine stitch down both edges of the Velcro. Remove all tacking stitches. (Fig.72)

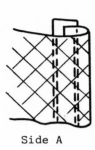 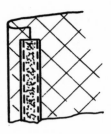

Side A   Side A

Fig.72

10. Starting at the underarm, bind the armholes in the same way as the pocket tops, but fold the end of the binding when you start to give a neat join as shown in Fig.73.

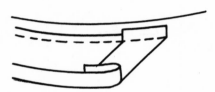 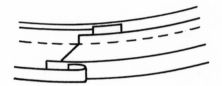

Fig.73

11. Starting at the lower side edge, bind all the way round the edge of the waistcoat, including the folded front edge. Fold the end of the binding when you start for a neat join.

JODHPUR PATTERN
(A pattern conversion)

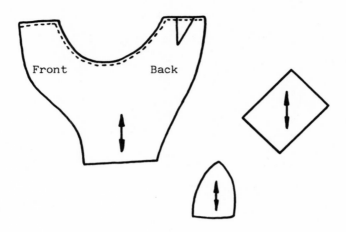

You will need:-

A pattern for a pair of tightly fitting trousers.

Scrap paper (such as newspaper or wallpaper) for the conversion stage.

Pattern paper or brown wrapping paper for the final pattern.

A felt-tipped pen.

Sellotape or pins.

Scissors.

To make the pattern:-

1. Place the pattern you are using for conversion against yourself, and ask a friend to mark on it the position of the below the knee seam of the final pattern for both the front and back leg pieces.

2. Place the pattern on the scrap paper, and transfer all the pattern markings, except the grain arrows. ESPECIALLY MARK "FRONT" AND "BACK".

3. Discard the original pattern.

4. Sellotape or pin together the inside leg seam on the scrap pattern, matching notches and seam lines as far as possible to keep the joined pieces flat. (Fig.74)

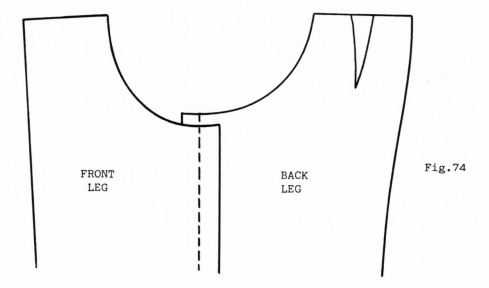

FRONT
LEG

BACK
LEG

Fig.74

5. Sellotape or pin together the outside leg seam from the lower hem up to the curve of the hip. Leave unjoined the hip shaping where this would prevent the paper from staying flat.

6. Mark and then cut the position of the new seam, starting at the unjoined hip part of the side seam, and curving to run down the front of the leg. This will cause the pattern to open out flat again. (Fig.75)

FRONT

Fig.75

7. Cut across where the under the knee seam is to be and mark new grain arrows as shown in Fig.76.

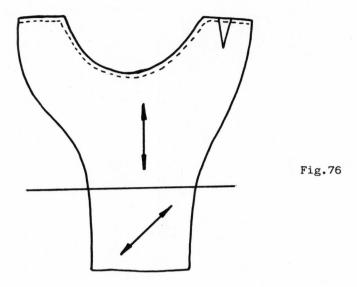

Fig.76

8. Recut the two new pattern pieces from pattern paper or brown wrapping paper, adding seam allowances to the new seam down the front of the leg and to the under the knee seam.

9. Transfer all the relevant markings to the new pattern pieces.

10. Cut out a suitably sized pattern for shaped knee patches as shown in Fig. 77. (About 10½ inches (27 cm.) by 6½ inches (16.5 cm.) for an adult.)

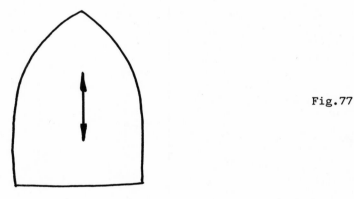

Fig.77

11. Cut a pattern piece for the waistband from that of the original pattern.

JODHPURS
(From your own pattern)

Although jodhpurs are fairly easy to make, some previous dressmaking experience has been assumed.

The pattern can also be used to make a pair of breeches by omitting the calf pieces and finishing off the edge under the knee in a suitable manner.

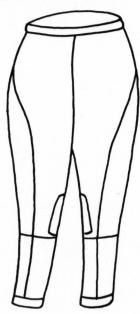

You will need:-

A pattern.

58 or 60 inches (150 cm.) wide stretch fabric the length of the finished jodhpurs plus 6 inches (15 cm.).

Waistband stiffening.

A hook and bar or a button for the waistband fastening.

A zip.

Matching sewing thread.

To make the jodhpurs:-

1. Fold the fabric in half down its length and find a suitable layout for the pattern pieces. Cut out one pair each of legs, calf pieces and knee patches. Cut out one only waistband.

2. Stitch and press darts.

3. Join the under the knee seams with a flat seam and then top stitch both
   sides of the join. (Fig.78)

Fig.78

4. Turn under and tack ¼ inch (0.75 cm.) all the way round the knee patches.
   Position these just above the under the knee seam near the back edge of
   the side/front seam and attach them with two rows of straight machine
   stitching ¼ inch (0.75 cm.) apart, or with one row of straight stitching
   ¼ inch (0.75 cm.) in from the edge and zig-zagging over the edge. (Fig.79)

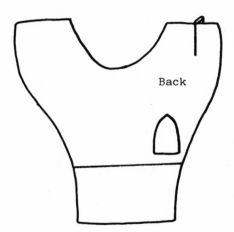

Back

Fig.79

5. Place right sides of the fabric together and join the side/front seam.
   Press it to one side away from the knee patches. Turn through to the
   right side, and top stitch the laid seam. (Fig.80)

Fig.80

6. Join, press open and insert the zip into the centre back/centre front seam, attaching a zip-guard if you wish. (This need only be zig-zagged or straight stitched close to the free raw edge.)

7. Attach the waistband and then the hook and bar or sew on a button and make a button hole.

8. Make a 3 inch (7.5 cm.) hem at the lower edge of the leg so that a cuff can be turned up when the jodhpurs are worn.

Optional extras

Strong elastic can be attached to the lower edge of the leg to pass under the instep.

A small coin pocket can be added, being sewn in with the waistband.

WATERPROOF HAT COVER

This could also be made in coloured fabric to identify members of a team.

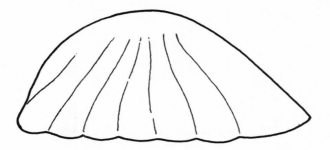

You will need:-

A piece of fabric 24 inches (61 cm.) x 18 inches (46 cm.)

¼ inch (0.75 cm.) wide elastic.

Matching thread.

A sheet of newspaper.

A felt-tipped pen.

A pin.

To make:-

1. Place your hat on the piece of newspaper and draw the shape shown in Fig.81. Mark the back edge of the pattern.

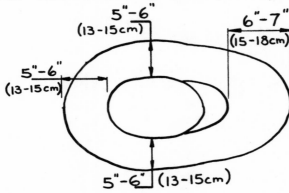

Fig.81

2. Cut out this shape in fabric, and use a pin to mark the back edge.

3. Turn under and stitch a hem which will allow the elastic to pass through, leaving a small gap through which to insert the elastic (Fig.82)

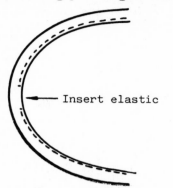

Insert elastic

Fig.82

4. Thread the elastic through the hem, and place the cover over your hat. Pull the elastic tight enough to that it fits snugly around the crown and under the peak of your hat, but loose enough for it to be removed and refitted when required.

5. To avoid an uncomfortable lump, stitch the ends of the elastic together when they have been cut to the correct length.

RAIN CAPE

You will need:-

Several large sheets of newspaper.   )
)
Sellotape.   )
)
A tape measure.   ) to make the pattern.
)
A pencil.   )
)
A piece of string about 1½ yards (1.5 m.) long.)

58 or 60 inches (150 cm.) wide proofed nylon (the quantity depends on the
   size of the pattern, and can only be decided when it has been made - step
   12 of the instructions).

A button or 8 to 10 inches (20 to 25 cm.) of 20 mm. wide Velcro touch and
   close fastening.

Sewing thread.

To make:-

1. Decide on the length of your cape by measuring from your throat to the
   top of your knee.

2. Sellotape several sheets of newspaper together so that you have a
   rectangular sheet 6 inches (15 cm.)wider than the length of the cape
   and 12 inches (30 cm.) longer than <u>twice</u> the length. (Fig.83)

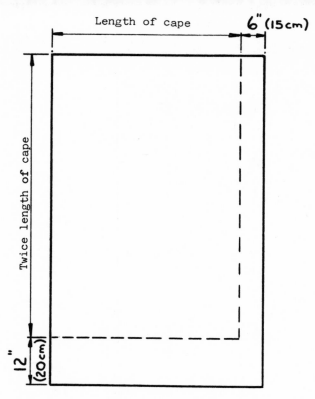

Length of cape   6" (15cm)

Twice length of cape

12" (20cm)

Fig.83

3. Fold the sheet in half to form a square. (Fig.84)

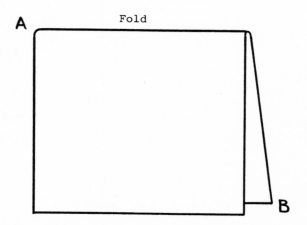

A   Fold

B

Fig.84

4. Fold corner A to meet corner B and firmly crease this fold. (Fig.85)

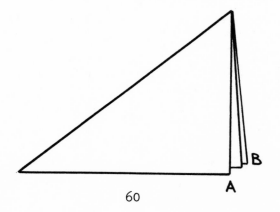

B

A

Fig.85

60

5. Tie the string around the pencil and hold the pencil point at position AB. Pull the string tightly and hold it at point X. Draw an arc from AB to C, and cut through the newspaper along this line. (Fig.86)

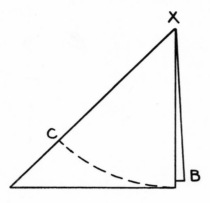

Fig.86

6. Using the same method draw another arc about 3 inches (7.5 cm.) down from point X for a child, or 6 inches (15 cm.) for an adult, and cut along this line for the neck. (Fig.86) More can be cut out later if required.

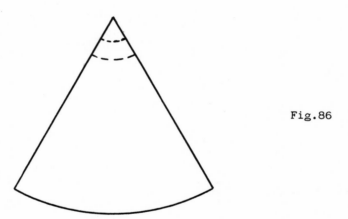

Fig.86

7. Unfold the paper once and mark the position where the folds were at the neck edge. (Fig.87)

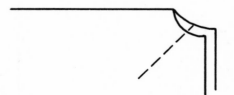

Fig.87

8. Mark darts about 4 inches (10 cm.) long from the neck edge along the two fold lines. (Fig.88)

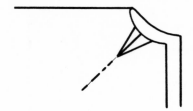

Fig.88

9. Cut two more strips of newspaper each the same length as the cape and about 4 inches (10 cm.) wide. Stick them to the straight edges of your pattern. (Fig.89)

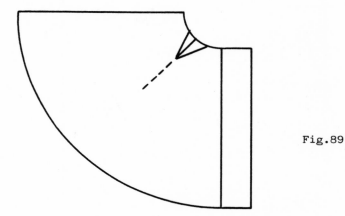

Fig.89

10. Open out the pattern and pin the darts in position. (Fig.90)

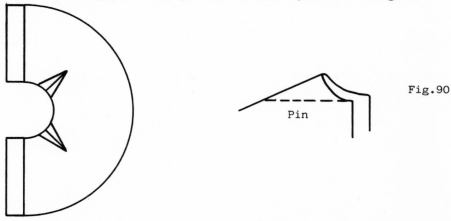

Pin

Fig.90

11. Try the pattern on. The strips of paper which you stuck down the
    front edge should overlap at the neck edge, and meet 8 to 10 inches
    (20 to 25 cm.) down from this edge. The pattern should not give the
    impression of being restricting, but should fit comfortably. Make any
    adjustments by adding to or taking away from the strips down the front
    edge. Adjust the position of the darts if necessary. (Fig.91)

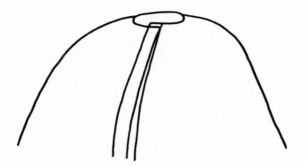

Fig.91

12. Remove the pins from the darts. Open out and measure the overall size
    of your pattern to decide how much proofed nylon you need. (Fig.92)

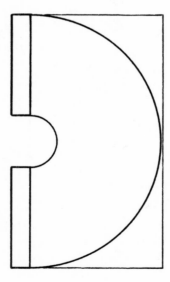

Fig.92

For a 36 inch (92 cm.) long cape the size of the pattern will be about
46 inches (117 cm.) by 84 inches (213 cm.). This means that the amount
of fabric needed is 2⅛ yards (2.25 m.). (Fig.93)

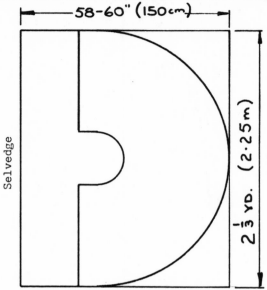

Fig.93

If the cape is 25 inches (63 cm.) long or less, it will probably fit
on to the fabric the other way and you will need about 1 yard (1 m.)
of proofed nylon. (Fig.94)

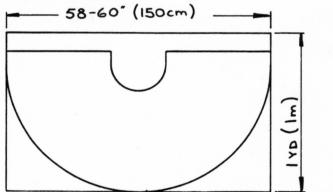

Fig.94

13. Cut out the cape, and with right sides of the fabric together, stitch
    the shoulder darts in place.

14. Measure the distance around the neck edge, and cut out another piece
    of nylon 2 inches (5 cm.) longer than the neck edge by 4 inches (10 cm.)
    wide for the neck band.

15. Place right sides of the fabric together and stitch one long edge to the
    neck edge of the cape. Make small nicks along the neck edge of the cape
    only. (Fig.95)

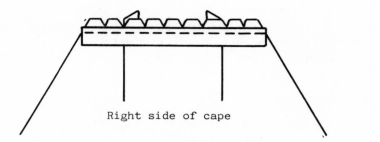

Right side of cape

Fig.95

16. Fold the neck band up and over to the inside. Turn under about ½ inch
    (1.25 cm.) along the raw edge and tack it in place along the first
    stitch line, but leave about 1 inch (2.5 cm.) at each end not tacked.
    (Fig.96)

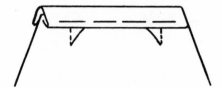

Fig.96

17. Place right sides of the fabric together and stitch up the front opening
    from the lower hem to within 8 or 10 inches (20 to 25 cm.) of the neck
    edge. Snip ¼ inch (0.75 cm.) at the raw edge about ½ inch (1.25 cm.)
    below the end of the line of stitching. (Fig.97)

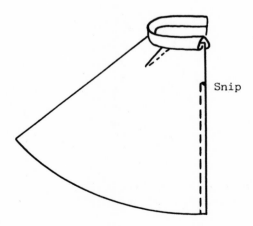

Snip

Fig.97

18. Turn in the ends of the neck band, and fold a narrow hem down the neck opening to the point where you snipped the fabric. Tack and then stitch from the top of the neck band to the lower end of the hem. (Fig.98)

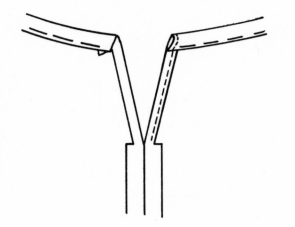

Fig.98

19. Stitch the inside edge of the neck band in place.

20. Hem all around the lower edge of the cape.

21. Sew a button on to the neckband and make a buttonhole at the other end of the neckband, so that this fits snugly, or mark the edge of the overlapping neck opening on the cape with chalk and sew Velcro touch and close fastening down the neck opening.

RAIN SHEET

This can be placed over your horse and saddle to keep them dry at shows, or for riding in wet weather. It does not need to be as deep as stable rugs so that your stirrup irons can protrude from beneath it.

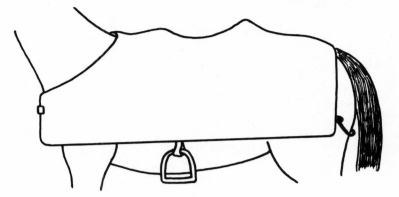

You will need:-

For a sheet up to 4 feet 10 inches (148 cm.) long:

 1½ yards (1.5 m.) of 58 to 60 inch (150 cm.) wide proofed nylon. (This is sufficient for a sheet 25 inches (63.5 cm.) deep.)

For a sheet more than 4 feet 10 inches (148 cm.) long:

 A piece of 58 to 60 inch (150 cm.) wide proofed nylon the length of the sheet plus 2 inches (5 cm.). (This will make a sheet 30 inches (76 cm.) deep.)

Sewing thread.

Optional: A nylon webbing strap and buckle.

To make:-

1. Fold the fabric in half down its longer measurement and cut out the shape of the neck. (Fig.99)

Fold

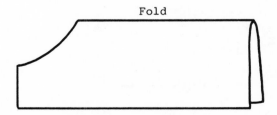

Fig.99

67

2. Turn in and machine stitch a small hem all the way round the edge of the sheet.

3. From the piece of material cut out from the neck, cut strips each 1½ inches (4 cm.) wide and join them together to form one long strip 1½ inches (4 cm.) wide by 2¾ yards (2.5 m.) long.

4. Fold the strip down its length and machine stitch close to the fold as shown in Fig.100.

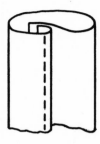

Fig.100

5. Cut from this strip 2 pieces each 4 inches (10 cm.) long and 2 pieces each 18 inches (46 cm.) long. Tie a knot in both ends of the remaining long piece to use as a fillet string.

6. Make loops from the two shorter pieces and stitch them near the lower back edge of the sheet as shown in Fig.101. Tie the fillet string to these.

Fig.101

7. Attach the other two pieces at the front edge to tie the front of the sheet together. (Fig.102)

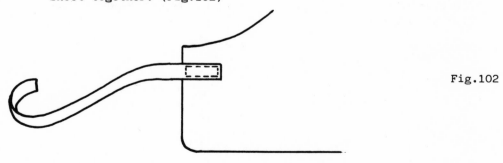

Fig.102

Alternatively, fit a strap and buckle to the front edge.

For riding boots with leather lining around the top edge only.

You will need:-

2 strips of thin, but stiff, black leather
each ¾ inch (2 cm.) wide x 4½ inches (12 cm.) long.

Strong black thread.

A harness needle.

A leather awl.

To make:-

1. Place one strip of leather, with the finished side against the inside of
   the boot, with about 3½ inches (9 cm.) of the strip above the top edge
   of the boot. (Fig.103)

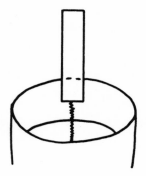

Fig.103

2. Use the awl to pierce holes through both the leather strip and the boot
   along the stitch line around the boot top. Back stitch the leather to
   the boot with the stitch overlap inside the boot.

3. Fold the leather strip down into the boot, and pierce and back stitch
   immediately under your first row of stitches about 1 inch (2.5 cm.)
   further down into the boot. (Fig.104)

Fig.104

BOOT JACK

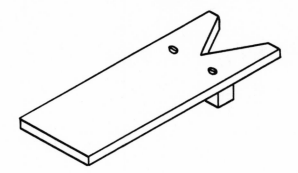

You will need:-

1 piece of wood 13 inches (33 cm.) x 5 inches (13 cm.) x ¾ inch (2 cm.)

1 piece of wood 5 inches (13 cm.) x 1¾ inches (4.5 cm.) x ¾ inch (2 cm.)

2 wood screws each 1½ inches (4 cm.) long.

Wood glue.

A screwdriver.

A saw.

A drill and bit to drill a pilot hole for the screws.

A countersink bit or bit slightly larger than the screw heads.

To make:-

1. Cut a 'V' in one end of the larger piece of wood as shown in Fig.105.

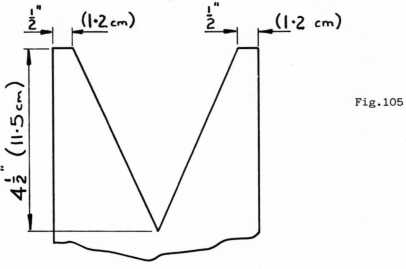

Fig.105

2. Glue the smaller piece of wood to one side of the large piece next to the 'V' as shown in Fig.106.

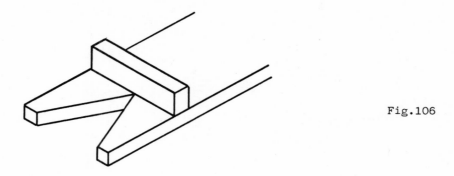

Fig.106

3. When the glue has dried, drill pilot holes for the screws from the top surface of the boot jack, through the large piece of wood and into the small piece underneath.   (Fig.107)

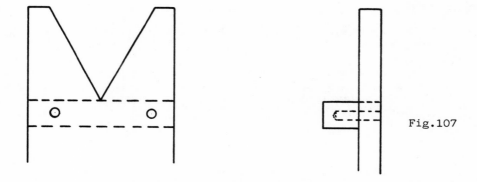

Fig.107

4. Using the larger drill bit or the countersink bit, make a depression to countersink the screw head.

5. Screw the two screws into the holes.

<u>You will need</u>:-

4 yards (3.75 m.) of ½ inch (1.25 cm.) wide tape in each of two colours (referred to as black and white).

A piece of dowelling ⅜ inch (1 cm.) thick and 54 inches (137 cm.) long. (The handle of an old-fashioned cob-web brush is ideal.)

<u>To make</u>:-

1. Fold the two pieces of tape in half and knot them together at the folded end. You will now have two black and two white tapes below the knot.

2. Place the knot over one end of the dowelling, holding it vertically. Arrange the tapes around the top of the dowelling so that the white and black are opposite their own colour. (Fig.108)

Fig.108

3. Taking both tapes of one colour in the same direction (e.g. both white tapes clockwise and both black tapes anti-clockwise) first pass each white tape under the black next to it, and then pass each black tape under the white next to it. (Fig.109) (Or, if you find it easier, pass black over white, then white over black.)

Fig.109

4. Continue winding tapes of the same colour in the same direction, and alternately passing white under black and black under white until the end of the dowelling or the tapes has been reached.

5. Holding the ends of the tapes firmly around the dowelling, slide the fillet string off, and knot the loose tapes together.

6. Cut through the folded tapes at one end and trim both ends neatly.

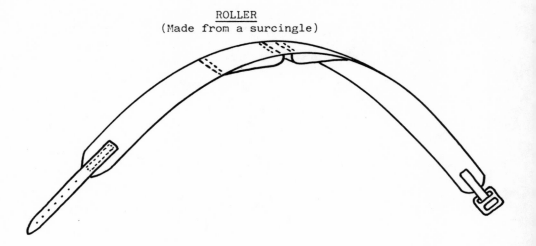

ROLLER
(Made from a surcingle)

You will need:-

A jute surcingle.

A piece of stout card the same width as the surcingle and 24 inches (36 cm.) long.

A piece of sturdy fabric such as cotton drill, denim or canvas, 14 inches (36 cm.) x 9½ inches (24 cm.)

1 yard (1 m.) of 1 inch (2.5 cm.) wide binding.

Soft toy stuffing or old nylon tights with the feet and waistbands cut off.

Copydex.

Strong thread.

A sheet of newspaper.

A ruler.

A felt-tipped pen.

To make:-

1. Establish and mark the position of your horse's backbone on the surcingle when it is done up.

2. Draw the shape shown in Fig.110 on the sheet of newspaper to use as a pattern.

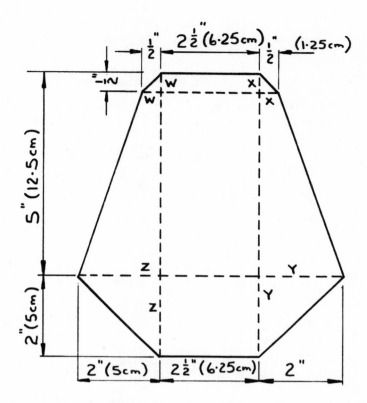

Fig.110

3. Cut out 3 pieces of fabric (A, B and C) using your pattern for pieces A and B as shown in the layout in Fig.111

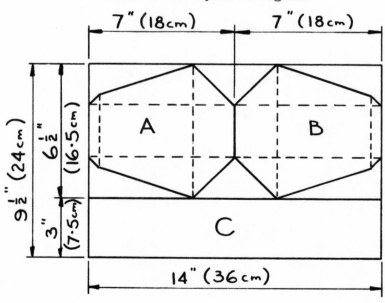

Fig.111

75

4. Mark the middle of the long side of the piece of card and line this
   up with the position of your horse's backbone marked on the surcingle.
   Stick the card to the under side of the surcingle.

5. Stick piece of fabric C on top of the card.

6. Fold and stitch the four corners W, X, Y and Z on pieces A and B as shown
   in Fig.112, leaving ¼ inch (0.75 cm.) at the raw edges unstitched.

Fig.112

7. Turn the resulting box inside out so that the raw edges of the corner
   seams are inside.

8. Places the two boxes on top of the card and fabric with the taller ends
   towards each other and a gap of 5 inches (12.5 cm.) between them. (Fig.113)
   ¼ inch (0.75 cm.) of fabric all the way round the edge of each box should
   be in contact with the card and fabric already stuck on the surcingle.

Fig.113

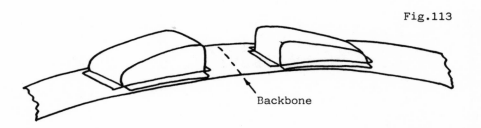

Backbone

9. Place a piece of 1 inch (2.5 cm.) wide tape across the surcingle at
   the taller end of each box to cover the raw edges and stitch through
   the tape, box, fabric, card and surcingle to secure the end of the box
   and cover the raw edge at the same time. (Fig.114)

Fig.114

10. Stitch along both sides of each box. (Fig.115)

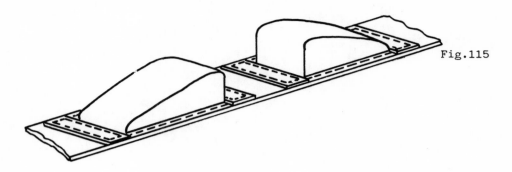

Fig.115

11. Stuff the boxes firmly from the outer ends.

12. Cover the raw edges at the outer ends of the boxes with 1 inch (2.5 cm.) wide tape as you did at the taller end.

13. Cut two pieces of tape each 1 inch (2.5 cm.) longer than the distance along the edge of the padded section including the width of the tape at each end.

14. Fold under ½ inch (1.25 cm.) at each end of the tapes and bind the padded section as shown in Fig.116.

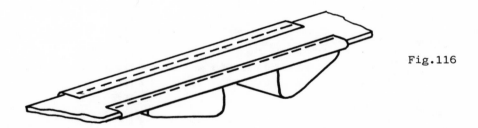

Fig.116

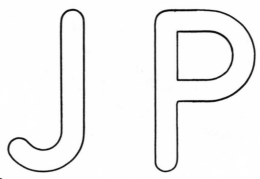

<u>You will need</u>:-

A piece of colourfast washable fabric in the colour of your choice large
   enough to fit your initials on.

A piece of fusible interlining the same size as the fabric.

Squared paper.

Dressmakers' carbon paper in white or yellow if the initials are to be
   dark, or a dark colour if they are to be light.

A pencil.

Sewing thread to match either the rug or the initials.

Tacking cotton.

A swing needle sewing machine.

Clear nail varnish if the fabric you are using is loosely woven.

<u>To make</u>:-

1. Draw the initials on the squared paper the same size and shape as you
   want them to appear on the rug.

2. Fuse the interlining to the back of the fabric you are using for the
   initials. This will help the initials to hold their shape after you
   have cut them out and minimise fraying of the cut edges.

3. Place the carbon paper between the fabric and the squared paper and draw
   around the outline of the initials so that this appears on the right
   side of the fabric.

4. Cut out the initials. Handle them as little as possible to cut down
   fraying. Although the interlining will help, if the fabric you have
   chosen is loosely woven some fraying may still occur. Painting the
   edges with clear nail varnish as soon as they are cut will lessen it
   further.

5. Position the initials on one side of the rug and tack them in place firmly. (Fig.117)

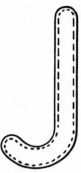

Fig.117

6. Select a zig-zag stitch on the sewing machine with about one sixteenth of an inch (2 mm.) between the stitches on each side, and stitch all the way round each initial on this side of the rug.

7. Select a close zig-zag stitch and go around each initial again.

8. Repeat with the initials on the other side of the rug.

FLEECY LEG PROTECTORS

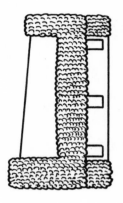 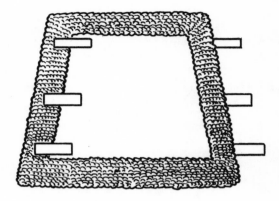

You will need:-

For a front pair, 2 pieces of each of the following for the size chosen:

	Large	Small
Cotton drill or similar fabric	17½ inches x 10½ inches (45.5 cm. x 27 cm.)	15½ inches x 10 inche (39.5 cm. x 25.5 cm.
¼ inch (0.75 cm.) thick foam	17½ inches x 10½ inches (45.5 cm. x 27 cm.)	15½ inches x 10 inche (39.5 cm. x 25.5 cm.
Simulated sheepskin	21½ inches x 14½ inches (55 cm. x 37 cm.)	19½ inches x 14 inche (50 cm. x 35.5 cm.)

For all sizes: 6 pieces of 30 mm wide Velcro touch and close fastening, each
    4 inches (10 cm.) long.

For a back pair, 2 pieces of each of the following for the size chosen:

Cotton drill or similar fabric	19 inches x 12½ inches (48 cm. x 32 cm.)	17½ inches x 12 inche (45.5 cm. x 30.5 cm.
¼ inch (0.75 cm.) thick foam	19 inches x 12½ inches (48 cm. x 32 cm.)	17½ inches x 12 inche (45.5 cm. x 30.5 cm.
Simulated sheepskin	23 inches x 16½ inches (58.5 cm. x 42 cm.)	21½ inches x 16 inche (55 cm. x 40.5 cm.)

For all sizes: 6 pieces of 30 mm. wide Velcro touch and close fastening, each
    4 inches (10 cm.) long.

To make one pair:-

1. Place a piece of cotton drill on top of a piece of foam and taper the
   sides by 1 inch (2.5 cm.) as shown in Fig.118. Repeat with the other
   piece of drill and foam.

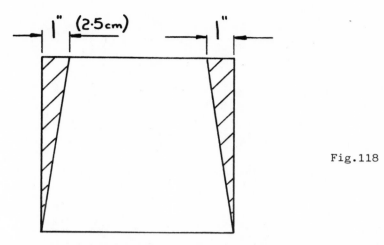

| 1" | (2.5cm) | | 1" |

Fig.118

2. Place the simulated sheepskin on the table with its pile side down. Put the piece of foam and drill on top of this so that the foam is sandwiched between the two fabrics. (Fig.119)

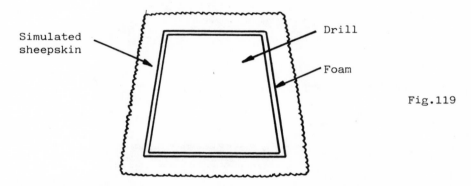

Simulated sheepskin

Drill

Foam

Fig.119

3. Fold the four corners of simulated sheepskin on to the drill, pin them in place and cut off the tip of each corner. (Fig.120)

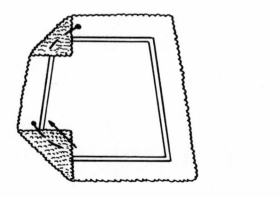

Fig.120

4. Fold the four sides of each protector over to the drill side and tack them in place (removing the pins from the corners as you go). (Fig.121)

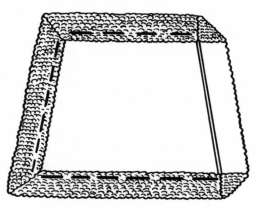

Fig.121

5. Machine stitch through all layers close to the edge of the sheepskin on the drill side. (Fig.122)

Fig.122

6. For each protector use three pieces of Velcro touch and close fastening. Separate the two halves of each piece, and stitch the three **looped** pieces on the left of the drill side for a nearside protector, and on the right for an off side, positioned as shown in Fig.123.

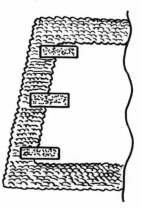

Fig.123

7. Stitch the loop pieces of Velcro on the sheepskin side, positioned to correspond with those on the drill side, with the edge of the Velcro overlapping the edge of the sheepskin by about 1 inch (2.5 cm.).(Fig.124)

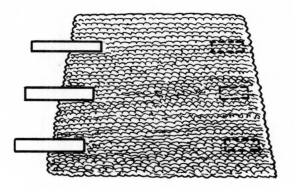

Fig.124

POULTICE BOOT

You will need:-

A piece of exterior plywood 2 inches (5 cm.) longer and 2 inches (5 cm.) wider than the sole of your horse's hoof, and ⅜ inch (1 cm.) thick.

A saw.

2 pieces of leatherette each 24 inches (61 cm.) square.

An adhesive which will stick the leatherette to itself and to the wood.

Strong thread.

A skewer and a leather boot lace <u>or</u> a knife and a leather strap long enough to go around your horse's pastern.

To make:-

1. Cut out the piece of plywood to the shape of your horse's hoof, but 1 inch (2.5 cm.) larger all the way round. (Fig.125)

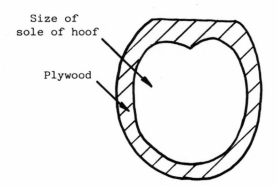

Size of
sole of hoof

Plywood

Fig.125

2. Place the piece of plywood at the centre of the wrong side of one of
   the pieces of leatherette, and then move it so that the straight edge
   of the plywood is 1 inch (2.5 cm.) nearer the edge. (Fig.126)

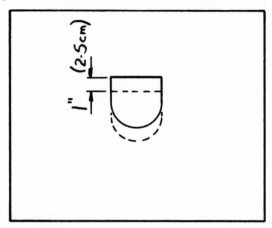

Fig.126

3. Stick the plywood in this position.

4. With wrong sides together, stick the other piece of leatherette on top,
   so that the plywood is sandwiched between the two. (Fig.127)

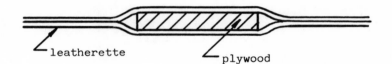

leatherette   plywood   Fig.127

5. Stitch through the two layers of leatherette around the edge of the
   plywood. (Fig.128)

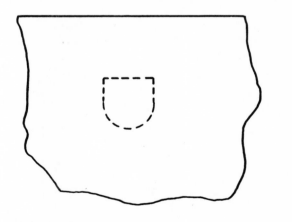

Fig.128

6. Measure the distance from the ground to just below your horse's fetlock joint at the positions shown in Fig.129.

Fig.129

A – at the front of the foot. B – at the side of the foot. C – around the heel

7. Add 2 inches (5 cm.) to each of these measurements and mark them on the leatherette by piercing four holes. (Fig.130)

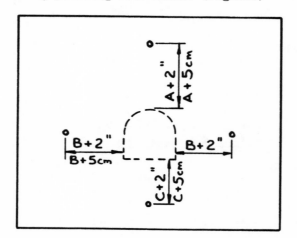

Fig.130

8. Stitch a dart in each corner on the outside of the boot to the measurements shown in Fig.131.

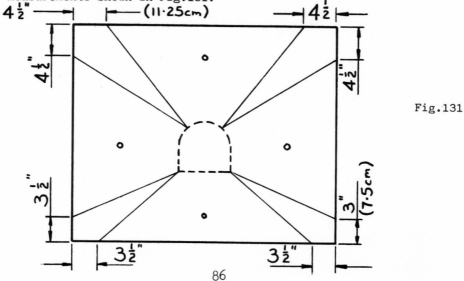

Fig.131

86

9. Cut off the folded corners to within ⅜ inch (1 cm.) of the stitch line. (Fig.132)

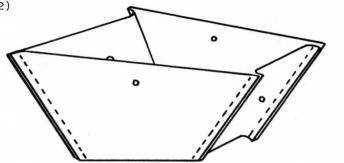

Fig.132

If the leatherette you are using is thick, you may need to make the darts larger to reduce the bulk around the fetlock. The opening at the top needs to be larger than the base so that a bandaged hoof fits in easily.

10. Make holes with the skewer if you are using a boot lace or cut slots if you are using a strap, around the boot using the four original holes as a guide. (Fig.133) There should be an even number of holes.

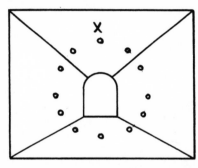

Fig.133

11. Trim the top of the boot so that there is approximately 2 inches (5.0 cm.) of leatherette above the holes or tops of the slots.

12. Thread the boot lace or strap through the holes or slots, starting at hole X in Fig.133.

When using the boot, it should be put on over the poultice and normal amount of bandaging – it provides additional protection, and does not replace bandages. Pleats should be formed under the boot lace or strap.

You will need:-

A piece of soft leather or leathertte 18 inches (45 cm.) x 12 inches (30 cm.)

A ruler or tape measure.

A felt-tipped pen.

Scissors.

Strong thread.

To make:-

1. On the wrong side of the leather or leatherette draw the lines shown in Fig.134, and then cut along them.

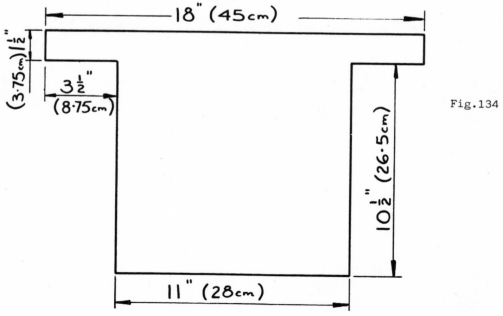

Fig.134

2. Fold the two short ends under and stitch as shown in Fig.135.

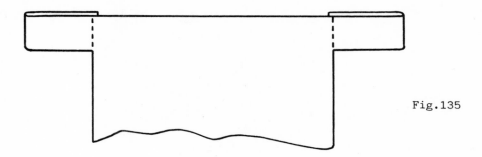

Fig.135

3. Make cuts to form a fringe about ¼ inch (0.75 cm.) apart as shown in Fig.136.

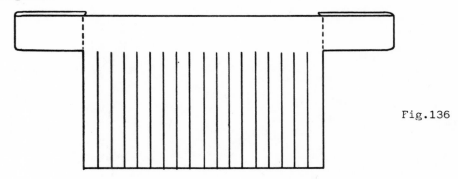

Fig.136

FLY FRINGE (2)

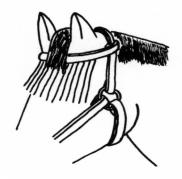

You will need:-

A piece of soft leather or leatherette 1½ inches (4 cm.) wide x twice
the length of your browband.

A quantity of baling twine.

1 inch (2.5 cm.) wide sellotape.

To make:-

1. Cut the baling twine into pieces about 10½ inches (26.5 cm.) long.

2. With the pieces of baling twine close together, place one end of each
piece on the sellotape until you have covered about 11 inches (28 cm.)
of the sellotape. (Fig.137)

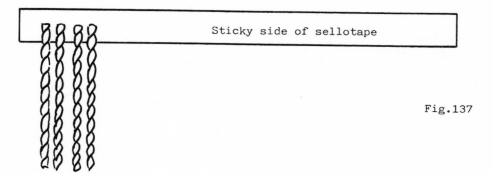

Sticky side of sellotape

Fig.137

3. Mark the centre of the strip of leather or leatherette, and find the centre of the sellotape. Matching these two points, place the sellotape on the wrong side of the leather or leatherette. (Fig.138)

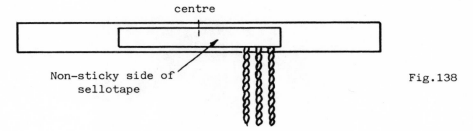

centre

Non-sticky side of
       sellotape

Fig.138

4. Fold the two ends over the baling twine so that they meet in the middle, and stitch as shown in Fig.139.

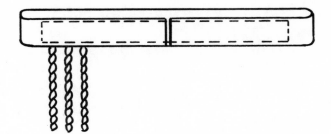

Fig.139

POLL GUARD

You will need:-

A piece of stout leather about 18 inches (46 cm.) x 2½ inches (6.5 cm.)

A piece of dense foam the same size as the leather and 1 inch (2.5 cm.) thick.

Adhesive to stick the foam to the leather.

A browband a size larger than you would normally use, which will fit the
   headpiece of your headcollar.

Strong thread, a leatherworker's awl, harness needle and a modelling knife or
   a woodworker's chisel the same width as your browband.

To make:-

1. Using the modelling knife or chisel, cut two slots each ½ inch (1.25 cm.)
   longer than the width of your browband, and two slots each 2 inches (5 cm.)
   long in the leather. Slot the browband through the smaller pair of slots
   and stitch it in place as shown in Fig.140.

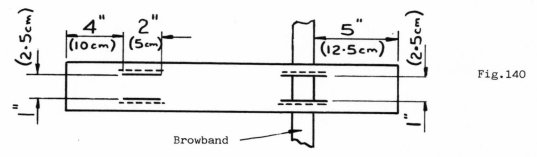

Fig.140

2. Stick the foam to the underside of the leather, making sure that the loop
   formed by the 2 inch (5 cm.) slots is not stuck down so that the headpiece
   of your headcollar can be slid through it.

TACK CARRYING BAG FOR BEST TURNED-OUT CLASSES
(To hold your bridle, stirrups, stirrup leathers and girth.)

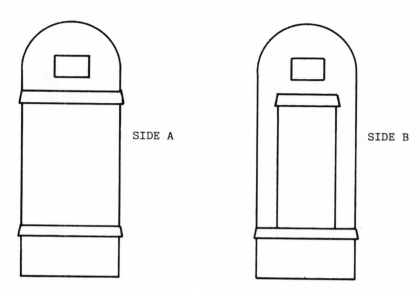

SIDE A   SIDE B

You will need:-

A piece of stout fabric such as drill, denim or canvas (or proofed nylon) 36 inches (92 cm.) x 48 inches (122 cm.)

16 inches (40 cm.) of 20 mm. wide Velcro touch and close fastening.

Sewing thread.

An 18 inch (46 cm.) zip.

To make:-

1. Cut out the fabric as shown in the pattern (one piece each of A, B, C, D, E, F, G, H, J and K).

2. Hem along one short edge of pieces C and C, and along one long edge of pieces E, F, G, H, J and K. Fold under and tack the opposite edges of all pieces and both long edges of piece D.

3. Place the wrong side of piece C on to the right side of piece A at the position indicated on the pattern, with the hemmed edge at the top. Stitch down both sides and along the bottom of piece C. Then stitch down the centre of it to form 2 pockets.

4. Stitch piece E on to piece A in the same way, at the position shown on the pattern.

5. Stitch pieces D and F on to the right side of piece B.

6. Fold over to the wrong side the long raw edge of pieces G, H, J and K, and tack these folds in place.

PATTERN E TACK BAG

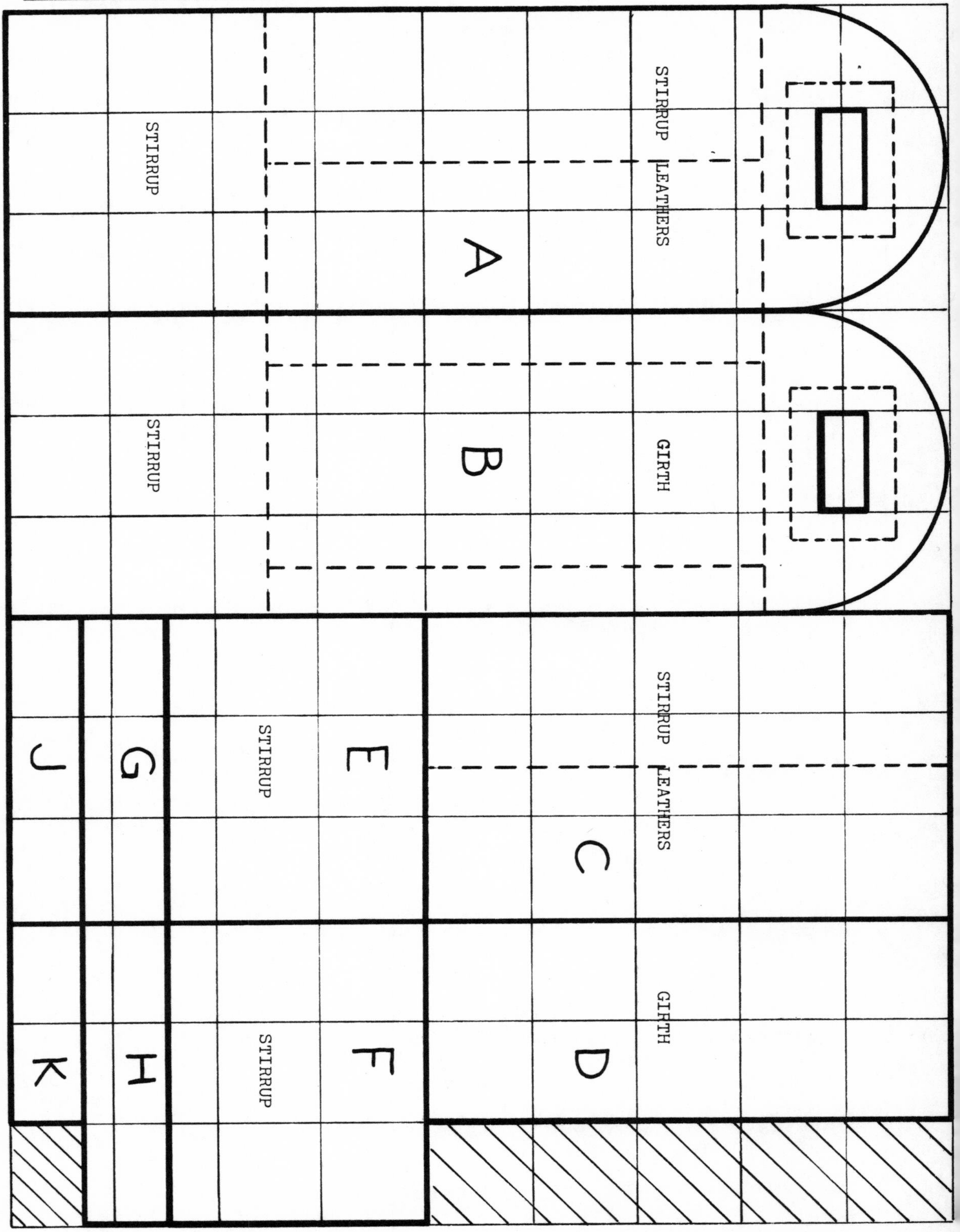
STIRRUP
A
STIRRUP LEATHERS
STIRRUP
B
GIRTH
J
G
STIRRUP
E
C
STIRRUP LEATHERS
K
H
STIRRUP
F
D
GIRTH

EACH SQUARE REPRESENTS 4 INCHES (10 CM.)
CUT AROUND SOLID LINE ONLY.

7. Pin and then tack these pieces at the top of each pocket, making sure that the entrance to each pocket remains open, and that the lower edges of pieces C and D are covered. (Fig.141) Machine stitch along the folded edge and both short edges. (Piece K goes at the top of girth pocket B.)

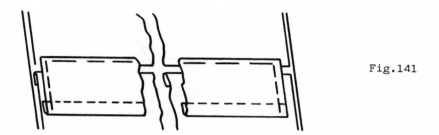

Fig.141

8. Cut the Velcro into four pieces – two each 6 inches (15 cm.) long and two each 2 inches (5 cm.) long. Fold in ¼ inch (0.75 cm.) around the opening which forms the handle on pieces A and B, separate the two halves of each piece of Velcro, and stitch all the hooked pieces on to the inside of piece A and all the looped on to the inside of B. (Fig.142)

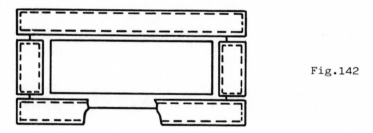

Fig.142

9. Place the right sides (with the pockets) of pieces A and B together, and, leaving the whole of the curved edge unstitched, stitch down both sides and across the bottom.

10. Turn the resulting bag through to the right side and insert the zip around the curved edge as shown in Fig.143.

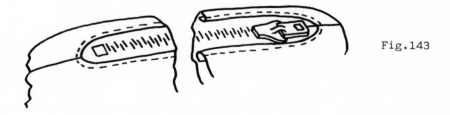

Fig.143

When using the bag, insert your bridle first and form a handle between the headpiece and browband by pressing the Velcro together. Do up the zip and hang the bag in some convenient place before putting the other items into their pockets.

95

PLAITING PINNY

You will need:-

A piece of sturdy fabric such as cotton drill, denim or canvas 18 inches
(45 cm.) square.

1¼ yards (1.25 m.) of 1 inch (2.5 cm.) wide tape.

½ yard (0.5 m.) of ½ inch (1.25 cm.) wide tape.

2 pieces of soft fabric each 3 inches (7.5 cm.) square.

Soft toy stuffing, sufficient to stuff 3 inches (7.5 cm.) square.

Sewing thread.

To make:-

1. Place the two soft pieces of fabric together and join them by stitching
   around three sides. (Fig.144)

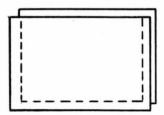

Fig.144

2. Stuff the space between the two pieces to make a pin cushion, and stitch the open edge closed.

3. Hem all the way round the piece of sturdy fabric.

4. Stitch the pin cushion at one corner of the main piece on the non-hemmed side, by sewing around all four sides of the pin cushion. (Fig.145)

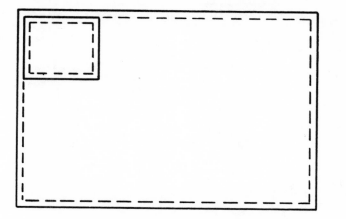

Fig.145

5. Place the fabric on a table with the pin cushion on the under side at the left lower corner.

6. Place your plaiting items on the fabric, and fold up the lower edge so that the pockets which will be made are deep enough to hold them securely but are shallow enough to enable them to be retrieved easily. (There will be a pocket behind the pin cushion which can hold something flat.) Pin between the plaiting items. (Fig.146)

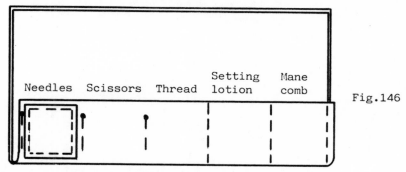

Fig.146

7. Stitch in place of each row of pins.

8. Insert your plaiting items into the pockets and fold down the top edge to cover them. Hold the top fold against your waist, and adjust the position of the fold until you feel that your plaiting items are at the most comfortable height for you to get at them easily. Mark the position of the fold with a pin at each end.

9. Stitch the piece of 1 inch (2.5 cm.) wide tape along the fold leaving
   two free ends to tie behind your waist. Stitch the piece of ½ inch
   (1.25 cm.) wide tape at its centre about half way between the waist tape
   and the lower edge of the pinny. (Fig.147)

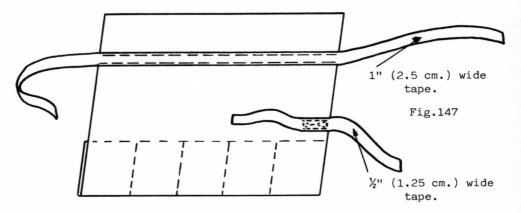

1" (2.5 cm.) wide
        tape.

Fig.147

½" (1.25 cm.) wide
       tape.

When wearing the pinny

Fold the piece above the waist tape over to the back before tying the pinny
round your waist.

When not using the pinny

Fold the piece above the waist tape over the top of your plaiting items.
Roll the pinny up starting at the end furthest from the ½ inch (1.25 cm.)
tape. When you have completed rolling it, wind the tape around the middle
of the bundle and tie the tape in a bow to store your plaiting things neatly.
(Fig.148)

Fig.148

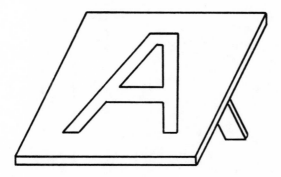

You will need:-

For each marker:

A piece of exterior plywood 12 inches (30 cm.) square x ⅜ inch (1 cm.) thick.

A piece of 2 inches (5 cm.) x 1 inch (2.5 cm.) wood, 12 inches (30 cm.) long.

A 2 inch (5 cm.) long hinge.

Screws for the hinge and a screwdriver.

Undercoat and primer paint.

White and black gloss paint.

Paint brushes.

To make:-

1. Paint all the wood with primer, undercoat and white gloss, leaving it to
   dry between coats.

2. Paint the letter or number you require on the marker with black paint,
   on one side of the plywood.

3. Hinge one end of the long piece of wood to the back of the plywood at the
   centre of the top edge. (Fig.149)

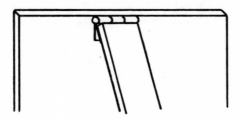

Fig.149

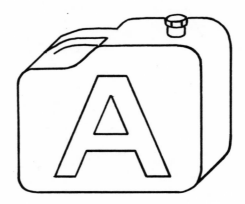

You will need:-

For each marker:

A 1 gallon (5 litre) plastic container.

Water, sand, soil or stones to weight the container.

White and black gloss paint and paint brushes.

To make:-

1. Thorough clean the container inside and out. Remove any labels stuck
   to the outside.

2. Paint the whole of the container, including the lid, white and leave it
   to dry.

3. On one side of the container, paint the letter or number required with
   black paint. and leave it to dry.

4. Weight the container by partially filling it with water, sand, soil or
   small stones and screw on the lid.

Positioning the markers around your arena

The letters required for a small arena are: A, B, C, E, F, H, K and M

Ideally a small arena should measure 132 feet (40 m.) by 66 feet (20 m.),
and the markers are positioned as shown in Fig.150.

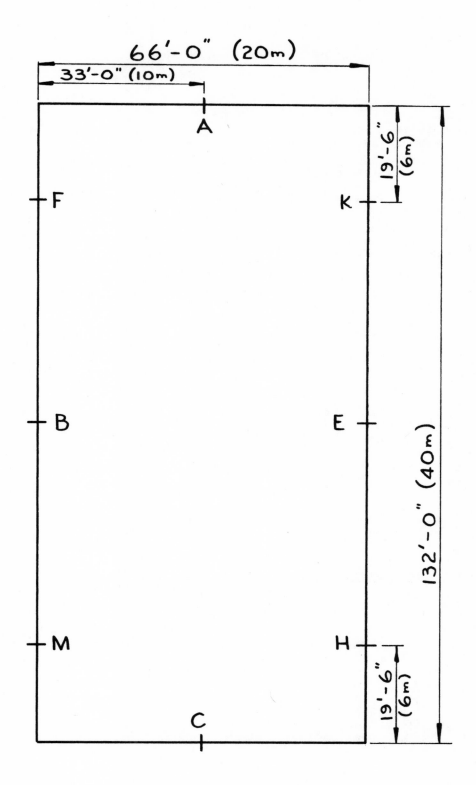

Fig.150

JUMPS AND JUMP WINGS

Jump wings

Except for the cross country type, jumps should be able to be knocked
down, and poles, planks, gates, etc. should therefore rest in such a way
that this can happen. Therefore, whatever you are using for the highest
part of the jump should not be fixed so that it cannot fall, and if a
spread fence is being built there should be sufficient room between each
part to allow the pole (or whatever else is being used) to fall to the
ground.

The following suggestions can be placed in various ways to give more than
one height (except the first), and you can probably add to this list:

Upturned bucket.

Straw bales.

Logs.

House bricks.

Celcon blocks.

Oil drums (these come in varying sizes and should be clean).

Barrels (these come in varying sizes).

Milk crates.

Wooden boxes (the largest probably being a tea chest).

Axle stands. (Ask father first!)

Easily constructed jumps

As a horse finds uprights (especially those without a ground line) the most
difficult type to jump, build only one or two of these, and if you have a
limited number of poles find something to use as a filler so that you can
build spread fences to encourage him to stretch. Make your jumps varied
and interesting, and rebuild them occasionally so that your horse does not
get used to going over the same ones time and time again. Build coloured
jumps as well as natural ones, so that he is not worried by colour if you
go to a show.

Nothing makes a horse more stale than continuously being asked to jump higher
and higher uprights, and he may eventually stop jumping altogether if this is
all he is asked to do.

Some suggestions for fillers under poles

Most of these could be used alone to make smaller jumps, but you should always try to include wings to make your jump look finished.

Straw bales.	Give a choice of two heights if laid end to end, and could have a pole resting on them or above them resting on wings.
Oil drums.	Large ones should only be laid on their sides, end to end.
Bags of manure.	Can be built up in rows or layers to alter the height and spread.
House bricks.	Should be restricted to one or two rows because they are rough and solid.
Celcon blocks.	Should also be restricted to one or two rows.
Plastic bottles.	Paint them to improve their appearance and use them in place of road cones.
Potted plants.	Should be non-poisonous to horses – definitely not yew or privet.
Tyres.	Should be firmly attached to a pole so that they hang below it. They can also be leant against straw bales or bags of manure.
A log.	Should have any branches cut off.
Garden trellis.	Fix this to a wooden frame, with the wood along one long edge protruding by about 3 inches (7.5 cm.) to enable it to be rested on a wing.
Brush.	Make the framework of a wooden box and fill it with brush.
Railway sleepers.	Restrict these to one or two rows because they are solid.
Milk crates.	Give a choice of heights.
Branches.	Preferably thin logs with any protruding branches cut off. They should be the same length as the width of the jump and three or four can be piled on top of each other.

Spread fences

Make spread fences from either two or three upright elements.

If you are using two, the second part can be the same height or higher than the first. If they are the same height only the first part needs a filler, but if one is higher than the other you can fill both, one or neither.

Three elements can be arranged in two ways (a) low, medium, high or (b) low, High low. For (a) filling is optional for all three, and for (b) no filling is required for the third part.

Some examples of home-made spread fences.

(A) House bricks and poles with Celcon block wings.

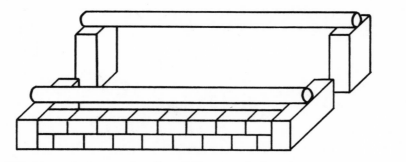

Fig.151

(B) Straw bales and pole with staw bale wings.

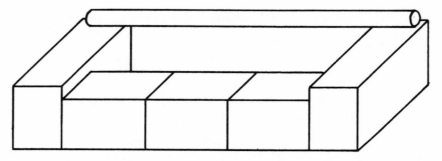

Fig.152

(C) Oil drums and poles with wings of Celcon blocks and oil drums.

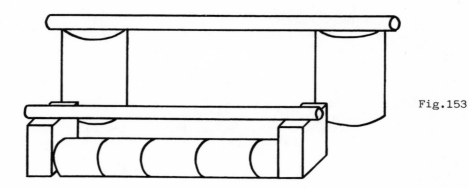

Fig.153

BITS AND PIECES

1. <u>A name plate for your stable door</u>.

   Rub Letraset letters on to a piece of wood and varnish it.

2. <u>Machine-washable bandage pads</u>.

   Use squares of simulated sheepskin. Thicker pads can be made by placing two pieces together with their pile sides outside, and zig-zag machine stitching them together around the edge.

3. <u>A whip tidy</u>.

   You will need three medium sizes baked bean tins, one with one end removed and the other two with both ends removed. Nail them one above the other with about 4 inches (10 cm.) between them, and the one which still has an end at the bottom, to the wall.

4. <u>Feed scoop</u>.

   Cut a plastic bottle as shown in Fig.154.

Fig.154

5. <u>Bending poles</u>.

   Grease the insides of flower pots. Fill them with cement. When the cement is firm but not set, stick garden canes into it through the holes in the bottom of the flower pot.

6. <u>Sausage boot</u>.

   Thread a leather strap through a piece of foam pipe insulation which has been covered with leather or leatherette,

7. <u>Bridle bracket</u>.

   Nail or screw empty sponge pudding (or similar sized) tins to the wall of your tack room to keep leather headcollars, bridles, cavessons, etc. from cracking.

HINTS AND TIPS

1. Add a couple of extra pieces of wood to an old wooden clothes horse and you have a collapsible saddle horse.

2. When storing leather which is not going to be used for some time, clean it, oil it, and then cover it in a thin layer of vaseline (including buckles and other metal). This will keep it supple and prevent it from going mouldy.

3. Use waxed whipping twine (available from boat chandlers) for your own leather work repairs. This will not rot and will probably outlast the leather!

4. Fix an awl blade as far into the handle as possible. Leave only about 1¼ inches (3 cm.) of the blade showing. This will bring your hand nearer the work and give you more control.

5. Stick an awl blade into the handle with a suitable adhesive to prevent the handle pulling away from the blade.

6. If your awl blade goes blunt, sharpen all four faces in turn on an oilstone. You can keep on grinding it away until it is about ¾ inch (2 cm.) long before you have to get another one.

7. If your hole punch goes blunt, sharpen it by running the blade of a penknife around the inside of the cutting edge.

8. If one of the punches in your revolving hole punch breaks, check to see if it is the type which has "push in" punches, by inserting a large nail into the back of the broken one and hitting it hard with a hammer. If it is this type, replacement individual punches can be bought. If it is not this type you have lost nothing by finding out.

9. Keep hole punches free of leather discs which get inside them each time you punch a hole. Clogged punches can cause the cutting edge to break.

10. Keep all old tack. The buckles and unbroken pieces of leather may be useful for repairing other items, e.g. part of an old stirrup leather may replace the headpiece on a leather headcollar.

11. A thin leather point needle in a domestic sewing machine for repairing rugs will pierce thick fabric better, and put less strain on the motor than a thick ordinary needle.

12. Clean your rugs thoroughly before repairing (or asking someone else to repair them) on a sewing machine. Any dirt on the rugs will get into the workings of the machine and will act like sandpaper on them.

13. When mending a New Zealand rug, stitch patches on to the outside of the rug so that next time the patches get torn and not the rug.

14. If the lining of your New Zealand rug is beyond repair, cut it out completely, and use a separate lining rug.

15. If the fronts of your rugs rub bald patches on your horse, stitch darts in the neck with the point of the dart at the point of the rub. Rugs rub because they are pulled tight against the horse's skin, either through lack of shaping or because the neck is too large. A dart will make the neck higher and provide shaping over the point of the horse's shoulder (think of your own bust). Drop the front strap if the horse cannot now get its head down comfortably - this does not make the neck too large again. Padding the front may appear to help, but it will not relieve the restriction on the horse's shoulder and will not, therefore, make the rug more comfortable.

16. Before using Gamgee tissue, zig-zag machine stitch along the cut edges. The Gamgee can then be washed and reused several times.

17. If the handle fittings break away from buckets, but the rest of the bucket is still good, cut new slots for the fittings at 90° to the original holes and refit the handle. (Fig.155)

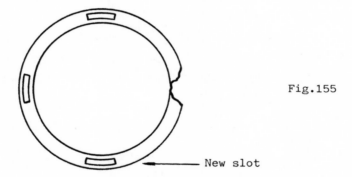

Fig.155

New slot

18. Fix two screw hooks about 2 feet (61 cm.) apart to the wall of your hay store at about chest level. Hook your haynet on to these to give you one hand free to fill it.

19. When building cross country jumps, tie them up with baling twine so that they are solid but can be dismantled and rebuilt in a different way.

SOURCES OF SUPPLY

Straps and buckles

These are often available from retailers specialising in leather craft work or outdoor pursuits.

Fabrics, binding, etc.

Suitable materials should be obtainable from fabric and haberdashery retailers and departments of large stores, or from markets.

Leather and leather working tools

Leather craft retailers should have these in stock or be able to get them to order. The smaller specialist shop often sells leather offcuts.

Woodworking items

Smaller D.I.Y. or hardware shops usually sell offcuts of wood at a reduced price as well as screws and other items singly, whereas the large discount warehouses sell only prepacked quantities.